BONSAI
- FOR BEGINNERS -

From Pot to Timeless Elegance. A Curated Collection of Ancient and Modern Techniques to Grow, Display, Compete, and Take Care of Your Miniature Masterpiece in 30 Minutes a Day

Kazuo Hanabusa

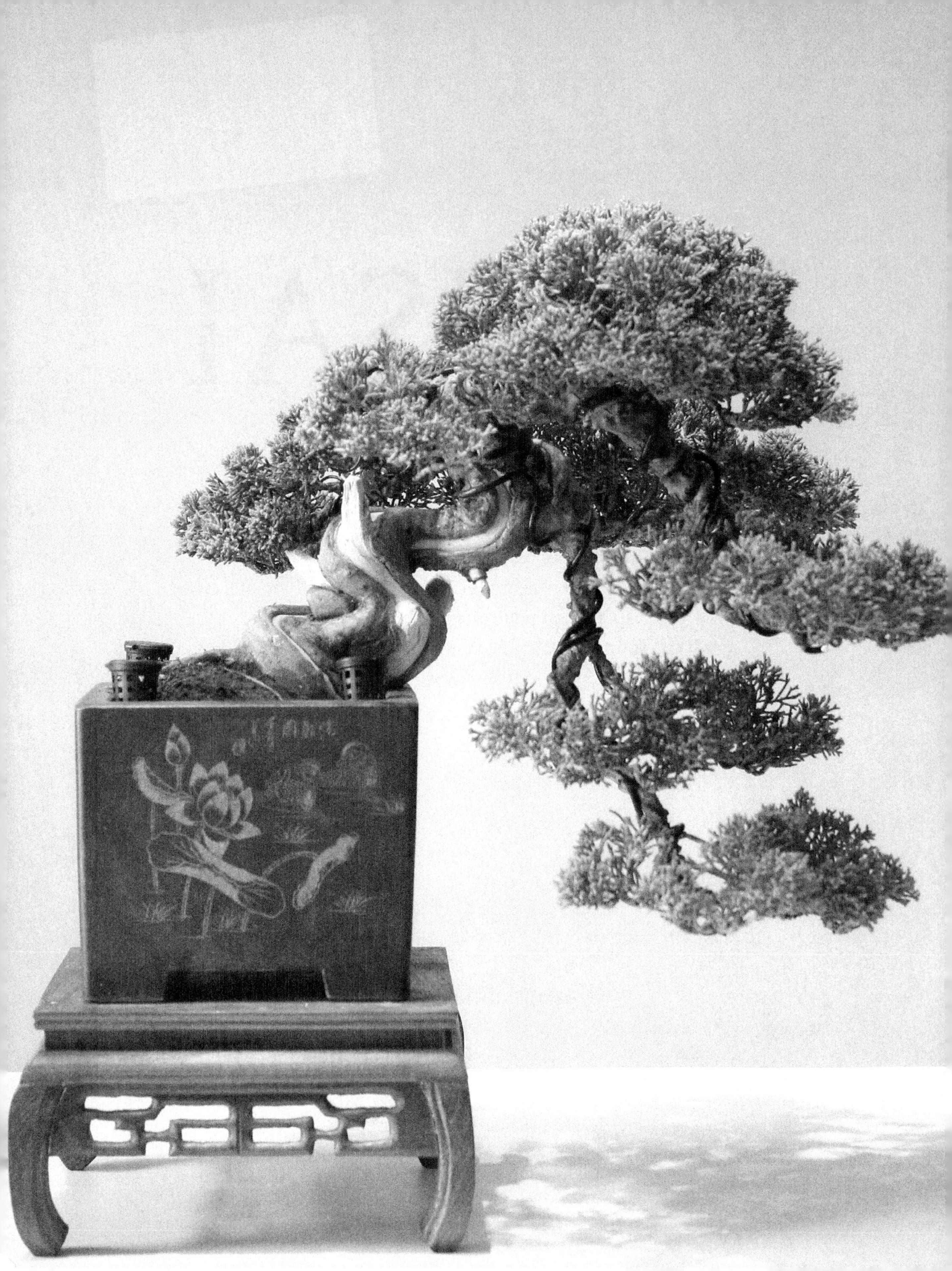

© Copyright 2023 by Kazuo Hanabusa - All rights reserved.

This document is geared towards providing exact and reliable information in regard to the topic and issue covered. The publication is sold with the idea that the publisher is not required to render accounting, officially permitted, or otherwise, qualified services. If advice is necessary, legal or professional, a practiced individual in the profession should be ordered.

From a Declaration of Principles which was accepted and approved equally by a Committee of the American Bar Association and a Committee of Publishers and Associations. In no way is it legal to reproduce, duplicate, or transmit any part of this document in either electronic means or in printed format. Recording of this publication is strictly prohibited, and any storage of this document is not allowed unless with written permission from the publisher. All rights reserved.

The information provided herein is stated to be truthful and consistent, in that any liability, in terms of inattention or otherwise, by any usage or abuse of any policies, processes, or directions contained within is the solitary and utter responsibility of the recipient reader. Under no circumstances will any legal responsibility or blame be held against the publisher for any reparation, damages, or monetary loss due to the information herein, either directly or indirectly.

Respective authors own all copyrights not held by the publisher. The information herein is offered for informational purposes solely and is universal as such. The presentation of the information is without a contract or any type of guaranteed assurance. The trademarks that are used are without any consent, and the publication of the trademark is without permission or backing by the trademark owner. All trademarks and brands within this book are for clarifying purposes only and are owned by the owners themselves, not affiliated with this document.

Contents

Book 1. Zen Bonsai Artistry | From Seed to Bold Serenity

1 What is a Bonsai?	7
2 The History of Bonsai	9
3 Why Everyone Needs a Bonsai: Benefits of Growing a Bonsai and What to Expect	13
4 Common Mistakes	16
5 Overview of Various Types of Bonsai	19
6 Choose the Suitable Bonsai Based on Your Time, Expectations, and Expertise	30
7 Be Inspired: A colorful Surprise	33

Book 2. Grow Your Everlasting Bonsai | From Soil to Perpetual Harmony

1 The 4 Evergreen Steps for Growing an Everlasting Bonsai	35
2 Tools, Equipment, and Materials	37
3 Preparation	57
4 Cultivation	67
5 Maintenance	77
6 Unlocking the Extraordinary: Elevate Your Bonsai Skills With Advanced Techniques — Your Exclusive Gift Inside!	91
7 A Wish From the Author	92

Book 3. Classy Bonsai Display | From Home Elegance to Eternal Fame

1 Introduction	95
2 The Importance of a Good Bonsai Display	97
3 Display Ideas for Your Bonsai	106
4 Feng Shui and Bonsai	126
5 Online and Offline Bonsai Competitions	127
6 A Gift to You: What Do You Want to Know?	134
7 Conclusion	135

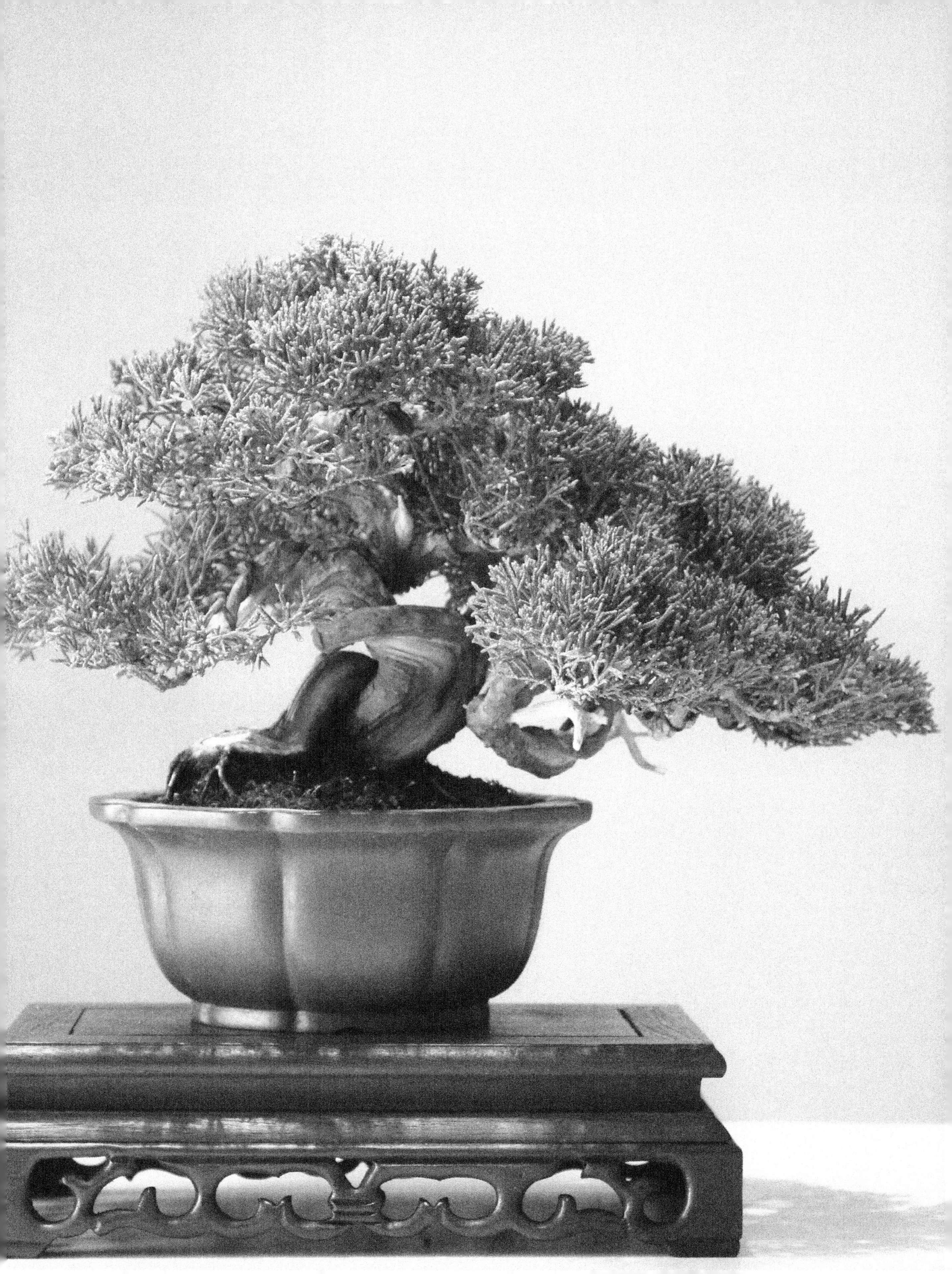

Book 1.

Zen Bonsai Artistry | From Seed to Bold Serenity

Discover History, Benefits, Common Mistakes, and Choose the Perfect Bonsai for Your Journey

Kazuo Hanabusa

1
What is a Bonsai?

A bonsai is an affirmation of life. It is a living thing, a work of art, and a labor of love. – Unknown

Have you ever encountered a miniature masterpiece of nature, nestled meticulously within a charming pot? I'd bet if you did you would be utterly captivated, maybe even spellbound, by this tiny marvel, carefully nurtured and exuding sheer beauty. It's almost too exquisite to touch and undoubtedly too mesmerizing to look away from.

That, dear reader, is the enchanting allure of a bonsai. Bonsai, often erroneously spelled as "Bonzai" or "Banzai," is a living art form encapsulated in a single phrase: "Planted in a container." Its origins trace back to the ancient practices of Chinese horticulture, but it blossomed into a unique expression under the influence of Japanese Zen Buddhism.

The term itself underwent a transformation to describe this Japanese art form, now represented by the intriguing characters 盆栽. At least we don't have to memorize the entire alphabet now. The first part of the symbol, 盆 (pronounced 'bon'), refers to a dish or shallow bowl. The second part, 栽 ('sai'), signifies a planted tree or another plant.

So, what's the whole business of bonsai all about? It's about crafting little tree replicas that look surprisingly real, without giving away the human touch. Contrary to what you might think, these trees aren't naturally dwarfed. Instead, it's a meticulous process that involves careful attention to wiring, pruning, nurturing, and crafting the tree's overall aesthetic. What's truly enchanting about growing a Bonsai is that you can use just about any tree species to create your very own piece of miniature horticultural art. Whether it's a deciduous wonder or an evergreen marvel, you have the power to craft a bonsai that embodies grace, harmony, and a sense of seasoned beauty. It's more than just a pastime; it's a true art form. There are lively communities and organizations spanning the globe, all united in their celebration of the splendor of the practice of bonsai.

The art of bonsai comes with the aim of maintaining each tree or plant at a height of no more than four feet. This is achieved by skillful container selection that restricts root growth and food storage capacity. The ultimate goal? To capture the essence of nature in a beautifully abstract miniature form.

Let's delve a bit deeper into the fascinating history of Bonsai.

2
The History of Bonsai

If you've ever found yourself lost in the captivating world of these irresistible miniature trees, you're most certainly not alone. Bonsai, the art of cultivating tiny trees that resemble their towering forest counterparts, has an incredibly fascinating history that spans centuries. So, without further ado, let's dive into the captivating history of bonsai, from its rich early origins to the modern-day masterpiece it has become.

2.1 A Glimpse into Ancient China

Our story begins not in Japan, where we often associate bonsai, but rather kicks off in ancient China. Imagine a world over a thousand years ago, where a deep appreciation for nature and the desire to capture its essence in miniature form led to the birth of this remarkable art.

Around 700 AD, the clever concept of "Pun-sai," which pretty much means popping a tree into a pot, took off in China. The idea was rather straightforward: pinch a piece from a gorgeous tree, give it a comfy spot in a pot, and watch it flourish in its own fascinating, tiny world. Initially, it was somewhat of an upscale hobby, mostly enjoyed by the elite of society. These potted wonders were even spread around as classy gifts, showing off a deep appreciation for nature's fascinating beauty.

At the same time, the Chinese also got all excited about something called "Scholar's Rocks." These were rocks shaped by nature into interesting, almost artistic shapes. People admired them not just for their visual splendor, but also for the deeper meanings they carried. This whole fascination with natural elements was rooted in the Chinese Five Agents Theory, which looked at water, fire, wood, metal, and earth as the core elements of the universe. This, combined with the desire to create tiny versions of nature, played a huge role in shaping the art of bonsai as we've come to know it today.

However, Bonsai in China wasn't just about appearances. The teachings of Taoism and Confucianism also had a great influence on how people approached bonsai. They believed in finding the perfect balance between humans and the natural world. So, tending to a bonsai tree also became a way to tap into that harmony and feel a real connection with nature. It was a way of living in harmony with our environment. It's pretty amazing how this ancient practice was about so much more than just growing trees in pots, right?

2.2 Japan's Zen Gem

Let's fast forward and hop on over to Japan, where the miniature bonsai landscapes found fertile ground as precious religious souvenirs during the Kamakura period (1185 to 1333). And it's right here that bonsai started to get that special Japanese flair we all recognize today.

Then there is the introduction of Zen Buddhism, which had a great hand at play when it came to shaping the Japanese perception of bonsai, making it an integral part of the quest for enlightenment and finding the path to inner peace. But it was not just limited to the monks or wealthy, bonsai trickled down from the imperial courts straight into the hands of commoners. All of a sudden nurseries sprung up all over the show and bonsai became synonymous with culture and refinement among the Japanese people. And the beauty is that it became accessible to anyone, granting they have patience and dedication for it.

As bonsai's popularity soared, five fantastical classic styles emerged, each with its own special charm, giving bonsai artists a framework for expressing themselves in their creations.

- **Chokkan**: the formal Upright Style
- **Kengai**: the elegant Cascade Style
- **Hokidachi**: the dramatic Broom Style
- **Shakan**: the windswept Slanting Style
- **Han-Kengai**: the dynamic Semi-Cascade Style

2.3 The Edo Period

Welcome to bonsai's golden age! The Edo period spanned from 1603 right through to 1868. It's a pretty big deal in Japanese history, also known as the Tokugawa period. This was a time of some serious action—we're talking political stability, a booming economy, and a significant boom in arts and culture. And, the art of bonsai was one of the shining stars during this time. Master artisans like the master haiku poet Kobayashi Issa were in their prime, creating masterpieces that still leave us in awe today. The whole bonsai game was stepped up. Bonsai wasn't just about sticking a tree in a pot anymore; it had become an art form, a thing of beauty.

The developments in bonsai during the Edo period laid the groundwork for its continued evolution into a refined and cherished art form in Japan. Bonsai's popularity continued to grow in subsequent centuries, snowballing until it eventually gained recognition on the global stage.

2.4 Bonsai Going Global

As the world shrunk through globalization, bonsai spread its wings and began to take root in other countries. Each place it landed added its own special twist to this ancient art form.

In the early 20th century, bonsai started flourishing its way to other parts of the world, all thanks to avid travelers and enthusiasts. The art captured the hearts of many far beyond Japan's shores, finding a new home in various countries such as the United States, Europe, and beyond. As it traveled, bonsai evolved, with each region adding its own unique touch. In the West, bonsai was embraced with open arms, but it also underwent a couple of changes. Aside from the art form merging with local flora and artistic sensibilities, it still remained true to the principles of bonsai, becoming a beautiful fusion of East meets West. This whole added fusion of Western creativity became a testament to the adaptability of this art form.

And with a big thank you to modern technology bringing us the internet, bonsai enthusiasts across the globe could further connect and share their love for the art form. With an onslaught of forums, bonsai websites, and, of course, social media, hubs to exchange ideas, techniques, and inspirations surged, propelling bonsai into a new era.

2.5 Bonsai Today

In our modern era, bonsai stands tall as an inclusive and cherished art form, embraced across continents. Whether nestled in the ancient landscapes of Japan or gracing the bustling streets of New York, these miniature trees continue to captivate hearts and spark inspiration. It's a timeless beauty that knows no bounds.

The journey of bonsai through the ages speaks volumes about humanity's deep connection with nature and our innate desire to capture its essence on a miniature scale. It's a practice that transcends cultural boundaries, uniting people from all walks of life. Bonsai isn't just about aesthetics; it's about forging connections. Whether you're a seasoned bonsai master or just starting out in this enchanting world, there's an undeniable sense of wonder at how these tiny worlds have left an indelible mark on history.

These diminutive trees serve as both a testament and a celebration of dedication and patience. They remind us of the intrinsic beauty that surrounds us in the natural world. With bonsai, beauty knows no limits. It's a testament to the power of human creativity and the boundless wonders that can be discovered in even the tiniest corners of our world.

3
Why Everyone Needs a Bonsai: Benefits of Growing a Bonsai and What to Expect

Isn't Bonsai something truly exceptional? It surely goes beyond simply cultivating little trees in pots. Sure, it's wonderfully captivating to look at, but it also has a slew of other advantages that go far beyond simple gardening. Let's talk about patience, for instance. Growing a bonsai is like a masterclass in dedication and time. It doesn't happen overnight, that's for sure. Despite this, people from all corners of the world are completely captivated by them.

3.1 But, Why?

But, why exactly do we love bonsai so much? For some, it's a deeply spiritual practice, a way to connect with something greater, for others it's sheer art. It's like having a slice of nature, vibrant and alive, right in your living space, and the reasons for this are as vastly different as people themselves. There's something about this art form that resonates with people for various different reasons from all walks of life. This makes bonsai a tailor-made experience which is what truly sets it apart. Bonsai transcends the typical houseplant.

3.1.1 What's in It For You

- **Stress reduction**: There's something magical about being surrounded by nature. It evokes a sense of calm. It's no secret that plants have a way of boosting our mood, and one of their benefits is reducing the stress hormone cortisol. So, having a little bonsai right there on your office desk isn't just about having a lovely view—it's a little stress-buster too!

- **Cultivates patience**: Compared to other houseplants, growing a bonsai takes time and dedication. The oldest bonsai tree in the world, a Ficus Retusa Linn of over 1000 years old, is a testament to this. Nurturing a bonsai is like nurturing a long-lasting friendship. As long as you tend to it, it'll keep thriving. Your investment of time and care isn't just for the plant; it's a gift to yourself. Your patience will grow stronger and more stable as you continually engage in this practice.

- **Generates self-awareness**: The way you care for your bonsai is a reflection of your inner reflection. Why? Your bonsai is like a mirror reflecting the care, affection, and gentleness that you hold within. It's a glimpse into how you respond to the world around you. And you know what's amazing? As your bonsai flourishes, so does your self-awareness. It's like a loop of growth and reflection.

- **Increases confidence**: Let's face it: caring for a bonsai isn't always easy. But seeing it thrive is undoubtedly a confidence boost. Its growth is a testament to your care and skill. It's not just a matter of choosing the correct approaches; it's also a matter of timing and precision. This entire process refines your problem-solving skills, exercises your patience, and increases your awareness. All of this, in turn, boosts your confidence.

- **Improved consistency**: We've all heard the expression "consistency is key," and it's entirely true! Your bonsai requires constant care that should form part of your regular routine. This is then accepted by your subconscious, fueling your consistency. Remember, the grass is indeed greener where you water consistently.

- **Teaches compassion**: That beautiful little miniature world needs care and compassion, that's the only way it's going to live longer. It's a process that instills compassion in us. Each nurturing session is a lesson, a cycle of growth and learning. Just as the bonsai undergoes its own transformations, so do you. It leads to a deeper fundamental understanding of the intricacies of life, fostering a greater sense of understanding and empathy.

- **Enhanced creativity**: Engaging in the art of bonsai unlocks your inner creativity. It sparks curiosity and encourages adaptability as you delve into a world of techniques and guidelines, each contributing to the uniqueness of your plant. It's a journey of self-discovery through artistry, where you get to explore your imaginative instincts and discover new ways to bring forth beauty and harmony.

3.1.2 For Your Environment

- **Air purifying**: Plants give us oxygen and clean up carbon dioxide through photosynthesis, effectively purging toxins from our surroundings. Let's talk about formaldehyde, for instance—it's sneaky, hiding in rugs, smoke, and even our grocery bags. But your bonsai works some good air-purifying magic. It doesn't just stop there, either. It also takes on other pesky bacteria in the air. Truly a gift from nature.

- **Humidity**: Plants play a role in balancing humidity levels, which is crucial for our well-being. Whether it's too damp or too dry, it can affect our health. Through a process called transpiration, plants release moisture into the air, helping to regulate humidity levels. And there's an added bonus! They also act as natural guardians, keeping materials like wood from getting too dried out in our homes.

- **Aesthetics**: Bonsais are living works of art, enhancing the visual appeal of any space. With their intricate branches and delicate leaves, they add a beautiful touch of natural beauty to any environment, creating a peaceful and visually pleasing atmosphere.

- **Cultural appreciation**: Growing a bonsai can lead to a greater appreciation for culture, history, self-mastery, and the art of bonsai itself. Growing a bonsai is an opportunity to learn about the traditions and techniques associated with its cultivation.

- **An heirloom**: Your bonsai can easily outlive you as long as it's in the hands of good care and dedication. When passed down through generations, it becomes a cherished family heirloom, a living legend, if you will. It stands as a testament to your devotion and hard work, leaving a legacy for future generations.

- **Symbolism**: Your tree might hold some powerful significance. Consider qualities like strength and resilience. As you nurture and craft your bonsai, you have the opportunity to infuse it with a unique story and meaning that resonates deeply with you. It can become a physical manifestation of your personal path and values, making it a really unique and personal creation.

These beautiful benefits are just scratching the surface. However, there's no need for further persuasion I'd say. Growing a bonsai promises not only personal enjoyment and a lively touch to your environment, it's a living legacy that can bring delight and admiration for generations to come, carrying on the love and art of bonsai through time. That's something truly special.

4
Common Mistakes

We're all bound to make mistakes, and your bonsai journey won't be an exception. That's perfectly fine! However, equipping yourself with ample knowledge beforehand can certainly smooth out a few wrinkles on the road ahead. Think of it as giving yourself a little head start in this fascinating bonsai adventure.

Let's have a look at some common mistakes that are easily avoidable.

- **Watering**: One of the most common mistakes: overwatering! Then there's the opposite, underwatering. It's crucial to get familiar with your specific species' watering needs. Some are thirstier than others. Also, don't forget to factor in humidity levels, as they can influence how often you need to water your bonsai. Too much water, and you're looking at potential root rot. Too little, and your tree's health and vigor could take a hit.

- **Sunlight**: Their requirements all differ. Placing them in an area with either too much or too little light will spell trouble. It goes beyond just growth. It also affects their ability to undergo photosynthesis, any plant's lifeblood. It could even lead to the unfortunate, final demise of your miniature tree. Think of it like not getting the right nutrients yourself—it's just not sustainable.

- **Soil**: It's of utmost importance to properly address the specific soil needs of your bonsai species. Using the wrong type of soil can mess with drainage and put your tree's roots at risk. Opt for high-quality bonsai soil that's designed for proper drainage, and steer clear of the standard potting soil varieties.

- **Potting**: Let's talk pots! Using the wrong size, be it too big or too small, is a surefire way to impede your bonsai's growth. The pot should always match the tree's size. And about repotting, that's a big deal in the bonsai world. Generally, it should happen every 2 to 5 years, but, yet again, it depends on the species. Getting your repotting technique perfected is crucial, it's one of the top culprits behind bonsai deaths. If you're unsure, don't hesitate to seek guidance from a pro.

- **Pruning and wiring**: Aside from harming the aesthetic of your tree, incorrect pruning and wiring are detrimental to tree health. It's wise to seek advice from a seasoned bonsai grower who can guide you in understanding your tree's unique needs. Keep in mind, in the realm of bonsai, pruning, and wiring are equal parts horticulture and art. Pruning involves an artistic touch within the realm of horticulture. But, bear in mind, one wrong snip, and your masterpiece could lose its luster. It's all about balance and precision.

- **Disease and pest control**: Like any other plant, bonsai trees may fall prey to pests and diseases. It's important to keep a watchful eye for any signs of trouble in this department. Neglecting this aspect can leave your beloved tree vulnerable to poor health or even demise. Familiarize yourself with the common culprits, like spring aphids, for instance. And when it comes to dealing with these unwanted guests, make sure you're armed with the correct methods to protect and treat your plant effectively.

- **Patience**: Lacking patience in this art is yet another big common mistake. Bonsai trees need their time to grow and find their footing. It's just like anything worthwhile in life, it demands a good dose of patience. Trying to rush things will likely result in stunted growth or the tree's demise. So, enjoy the journey. Remember, even Rome wasn't built in a day.

- **Regular maintenance**: Never ever underestimate the power of consistent care. It's all about giving your bonsai the time and attention it requires to fully flourish into the miniature beauty it ought to. Tasks like pruning, wiring, and repotting, when done correctly and regularly, play a crucial role in ensuring your bonsai thrives for the long haul. It's all part of the sustainability package in the world of bonsais.

- **The basics**: Knowledge is definitely power in the world of bonsai, and understanding bonsai basics is key. This covers everything from design principles to care, maintenance, different species, and exploring various styles. It's important to have a solid grasp of what you're doing when you're tending to your tree. Skipping out on research can easily lead to unintended slip-ups and a fair bit of frustration down the line.

- **Aesthetic balance**: Undoubtedly this is a crucial aspect of bonsai care, woven right into the fabric of the art form. Grasping those subtle details of harmonious aesthetic design is pivotal in nurturing a bonsai that's not only visually appealing but also maintains that natural charm. After all, life's about finding that perfect balance, and it's no different when it comes to your bonsai.

You can take proactive steps to avoid these common mistakes and provide the best possible care for your miniature trees. Remember, every mistake is an opportunity to learn and grow, especially in the art of bonsai cultivation.

5
Overview of Various Types of Bonsai

Enchanting bonsai trees with their miniature forms, come in a delightful array of styles, each with its own special charm. These styles reflect the diverse environments and natural conditions that have influenced the growth of these remarkable trees. So, let's take a dive into a couple of the most prominent and captivating types of bonsai.

5.1 Formal Upright/Chokkan

One of the most familiar bonsai styles: is the Formal Upright, or Chokkan. It's like nature's own little version of a skyscraper. The trunk rises straight, radiating a sense of balance and vigor. It's as if it's been meticulously designed with a perfect taper to the top. At the pinnacle, a single branch extends to form the crown. And here's an important detail: the trunk should be heavier at the base, gradually tapering and thinning as it stretches towards the top.

5.2 Informal Upright/Moyogi

This organic, free-flowing posture lends it a natural charm, often mirroring the organic shapes we find in nature.

Along its course, you'll notice branches sprouting, each one adding to its character, and yet again with the trunk tapering thinner towards the top.

5.3 Slanting/Shakan

Imagine a tree growing on a mountainside, its trunk leaning against the slope and reaching for the sunlight. That's the essence of the Slanting style.

The trunk takes on an angle, usually between 60 to 80 degrees, creating a dynamic sense of movement. This tilt occurs because the roots on one side of the tree grow stronger compared to the side it leans towards. The trunk might have a subtle bend or remain almost straight, but it maintains a thicker base, tapering gradually as it ascends.

5.4 Cascade/Kengai

This style emulates a tree that has braved the elements on a cliff edge, with its branches cascading downward.

It's a powerful portrayal of nature's ability to endure and adapt. Cultivating this style in bonsai art can be quite a challenge, requiring a keen understanding of balance and form.

5.5 Semi-Cascade/Han-Kengai

The semi-cascade bonsai merges the best of both worlds, blending elements of both the upright and cascade styles. It's like a delightful meeting point.

In this style, you'll notice that the trunk never extends below the bottom of the pot. Instead, the crown typically rises above the pot's rim, with branching elegantly cascading below.

5.6 Windswept/Fukinagashi

Picture a tree that's stood resilient against some fierce winds, its branches and leaves swept in a testament to its battle for survival.

Over time, each branch gets bent towards one side of the trunk, creating this particular aesthetic that beautifully reflects struggle and endurance.

5.7 Broom/Hokidachi

This style works wonders for trees with abundant, delicate branches, presenting a distinct air of order and formality.

Picture an upright trunk with branches spreading out in a balanced, broom-like manner, ultimately forming a crown that resembles a sphere. Nature's way of showcasing meticulous craftsmanship.

5.8 Group Planting/Yose-ue

Here, multiple trees are planted together, creating a harmonious miniature forest scene. It's like a snapshot of nature's own woodland with the multi-trunk style of various trees.

The more mature and developed trees are strategically placed at the center, while smaller ones gracefully fringe the outskirts in a staggered arrangement, adding an authentic touch to the scene.

5.9 Multi-Trunk/Ikadabuki

In this style, we observe multiple trunks springing from a common root system. It's a reflection of how trees naturally grow in dense forests, where several trunks ascend together, benefiting from a shared nutrient supply.

This collective effort results in the creation of one magnificent, unified canopy.

5.10 Bonsai on Rock/Ishizuki

This style really emphasizes the bonsai's connection with nature. The tree is nestled on a rock, its roots intertwining with the stone, blending the organic and inorganic in a beautiful visual union. Now, it's worth noting that this style does demand a bit more attention. Rocks don't offer much room for storing water and nutrients, so you'll need to be diligent with watering and fertilizing. That's why, typically, this style is planted in low, shallow pots, often filled with water or fine gravel to ensure the tree gets enough nourishment.

These are just the tip of the iceberg of the many captivating styles that you may explore. Each style has its own unique story, capturing a moment in life as it reflects the diverse landscapes and conditions that shape them.

So, whether you're drawn to the strength and symmetry of the formal upright, or the rugged resilience of the cascade, there's a bonsai style for all of us, perhaps even more than one. It's a journey of exploration, learning, and creativity, where you get to shape and nurture your own miniature natural wonder. Isn't that just fascinating?

5.11 Need More Inspiration?

The world of bonsai has seen some remarkable figures, but few have left a mark as indelible as Master Kimura. Renowned as the "Magical Technician of Kindai Shuppan, who dared to challenge conventions and redefined bonsai artistry. Kimura's creations, especially those fashioned from Shimpaku junipers, blur the lines between tree and art, inviting us into a realm of almost surreal beauty.

Then there is the infamous championing Ezo Spruce Bonsai Forset maestro, Saburo Kato. This luminary legend in the world of bonsai, carved his legacy as the father of Ezo spruce bonsai. With a profound respect for nature, Saburo advocated for compositions of multiple trees in a single planting. Kunio Kobayahi, the grand master when it comes to fusing modernism and tradition, his philosophy captures the spiritual essence of trees, embodying the wabi-sabi ethos of Japanese culture. Kunio's meticulous detailing and dynamic compositions breathe life into his bonsai, showcasing the raw beauty of nature.

Let us bridge cultures with various ambassadors of the art of bonsai, each bringing their unique perspective. From Michael Hagedorn's naturalistic approach to Koji Hiramatsu's captivating forest compositions. These artists are not only shaping bonsai but also bridging cultures through their shared passion.

Scan your QR code below to become inspired by the masters of this art!

6
Choose the Suitable Bonsai Based on Your Time, Expectations, and Expertise

Even with its intricate beauty and profound symbolism, selecting the right bonsai isn't just all about aesthetics. It involves considering your lifestyle, aspirations, and expertise level—factors that hold the key to your success in this endeavor. We'll explore how to choose the perfect bonsai based on your time, expectations, and expertise.

6.1 Expectations

Your unique expectations and vision for your bonsai play a significant role when it comes to selecting the perfect tree for you. Let's delve into some valuable insights that can help guide you in making this important decision.

- **For elegance and strength**: The Formal Upright style, with its straight, symmetrical trunk, exudes a sense of order and strength, grace, and resilience.

- **For a miniature forest**: For a snapshot of nature's own woodland, consider the Group Planting style. with multiple trunks growing together to form a serene and captivating scene you can create your own indoor miniature forest.

- **For resilience and adaptability**: The Cascade style emulates trees that have endured harsh conditions on cliff edges. With their branches gracefully cascading downwards, a striking portrayal of nature's ability to adapt and thrive introduces captivating curves and shapes to your surroundings.

- **For natural beauty**: The Informal Upright style brilliantly reflects nature's naturalistic, unstrained postures. It portrays the natural beauty of trees that have survived the elements and endured the test of time with their delicate twists and curves.

6.2 Time

One of the most critical factors in choosing a bonsai is the amount of time you can dedicate to its care. Bonsai, like any living entity, requires consistent care and attention. Different species have different needs, so it's important to match your availability with your chosen tree's requirements.

- **High maintenance**: If you're more determined and prepared to invest substantial amounts of time and effort, more fragile species like the Trident Maple may be ideal for you. These trees require stringent maintenance, such as precise watering, regular pruning, and a close eye on monitoring of their environment.

- **Moderate maintenance**: If you have a little more time or are at an intermediate level, species like Juniper or Chinese Elm can be a good move forward. You can appreciate the art of bonsai without making too many commitments by striking a balance between hardiness and the requirement for frequent care.

- **Low-maintenance**: If your lifestyle is on the busy side of things with a packed schedule and limited, consider low-maintenance bonsai species like the Jade or Ficus for instance. They are forgiving and sturdy trees that can survive with less frequent irrigation and pruning.

6.3 Expertise Level

Your level of expertise in bonsai is another yet another important factor up for consideration. Naturally, beginners may find certain species more forgiving, while experienced enthusiasts can take on more challenging varieties.

- **Beginner species**: For those new to bonsai, you will be looking for species that are more forgiving and provide an excellent, encouraging starting point. They're generally more resilient which is exactly what makes them ideal for honing your skills.

- Ficus
- Jade
- Rosemary
- Juniper
- Portulacaria

- **Intermediate species**: As you gain confidence and experience, you can opt for species that offer a more intricate challenge, allowing you to refine your techniques and hone your craft.
    - Boxwood
    - Pine
    - Beech
    - Cotoneaster

- **Advanced species**: Seeking the pinnacle of challenge? Delicate species like the Japanese White Pine can be incredibly rewarding. These trees demand an advanced level of skill, expertise, and, of course, time and patience.
    - Cherry Blossom
    - Bamboo
    - Gardenia
    - Cedar
    - Buttonwood

Choosing a bonsai isn't merely about quickly choosing a new plant, it's a personal decision that transcends mere aesthetics. It involves discovering a living masterpiece that harmonizes with your way of life, skill level, and environment. When you take into account your schedule, hopes, and experience, you'll be embarking on a bonsai adventure that's deeply satisfying. Always remember, bonsai isn't just a hobby, it's an enduring connection with the natural world. It's a gratifying commitment that culminates in the ageless allure of a living masterpiece.

7
Be Inspired: A Colorful Surprise

Propel your expert level of mastery in your bonsai journey by diving straight into the world of bonsai in full color! What exactly am I referring to?
A delightful extra; you'll stumble upon a QR code in this chapter, granting you free access to its contents in full color!

We're fully aware of the constraints of the black-and-white version of any book. That's precisely why we're offering the color version at no extra cost. But hold on a second, there's even more to come! In the subsequent books of this series, we'll unravel two additional surprises, enhancing your enchanting journey even further. So, let's venture forth on this exhilarating artistic pursuit together! Bonsai knows no borders! This is just the tip of the bonsai iceberg, offering a wealth of inspiration. Whether you're a beginner or a seasoned enthusiast. So, let's dive into this global community, where passion for bonsai transcends borders.

Book 2.

Grow Your Everlasting Bonsai | From Soil to Perpetual Harmony

Tools, Preparation, Cultivation, Maintenance, and Revitalization.
Techniques for a Healthy, Well-Groomed Bonsai

Kazuo Hanabusa

1
The 4 Evergreen Steps for Growing an Everlasting Bonsai

So, you want a splendid little tree displayed in all its glory in some nook of your space, right? I most certainly can't blame you, after all, who wouldn't be captivated? I have to warn you though, once you cross that threshold and step into the world of Bonsai, there's no turning back!

We're all rendered powerless against the charm and enchantment these miniature wonders exude. Take one home, and you'll undoubtedly amplify the joy in your surroundings. But with such great beauty and privilege comes responsibility.

Fret not, this responsibility is integral to mastering the art of bonsai, the same way a painter masters his brushstrokes and hues. After all, it requires patience, care, and unwavering dedication to produce a masterpiece of any sort.

Thus, you are at the right place at the right time, my fellow bonsai enthusiast. Here we're going to step it a notch up and delve into what you need to create your own miniature masterpiece.

We'll be honing in on the tools you require, cultivation, maintenance, and let me not forget, a delightful surprise for you.

Without further ado, let's get started with this fascinating journey!

2
Tools, Equipment, and Materials

By now, it's no secret that getting into the world of bonsai calls for patience, dedication, and, of course, the right know-how. This means having the proper tools, prepping like a pro, and tending to your bonsai with the utmost care in order to keep it flourishing and showcasing your newly honed skills and perfected artistry. Now, let's delve into some steps that will help you create a legendary, standout miniature tree.

2.1 Overview

In life, we always have choices, and it's no different when it comes to picking out tools for your bonsai adventure. It's pretty much a case of "you get what you pay for." There's the pricier option, which naturally offers better quality compared to the cheaper, lower-end options. However, you don't need to go all out and empty your bank account to get stocked up for the endeavor. You can start small if necessary and gradually expand your collection with time.

You will come across two different steel varieties for bonsai tools: stainless steel and carbon steel. Carbon steel is known for its durability and sharpness, which is a big deal when you're dealing with delicate branches. Carbon steel tools can hold an edge really well, making them a favorite among bonsai enthusiasts who appreciate precision. And Japanese Carbon steel takes this one step further, with its incredible strength it is also why you'll find the best chef knives and swords made from it. But, there's a tiny catch. Carbon steel tools can be a tad prone to rust due to the lack of chromium if they're not dried properly and oiled after use. However, be wary because if it's not Japanese Carbon steel, steer clear as there are a lot of companies that make the claims, however, it's made out of alloy.

Stainless steel tools are resistant to rust, thus they are more forgiving if you forget to wipe them down after a session.

Now, here's the thing, while stainless steel is a champ at resisting corrosion, it might not hold an edge quite as long as carbon steel. So, there's a bit of a trade-off. You might need to sharpen them a bit more often in exchange for the convenience.

Ultimately, the choice between carbon and stainless steel comes down to your personal preference, price point, and how you plan to care for your tools. Either way, both materials have their strengths and can serve you well in your bonsai endeavors.

A handy tip to make sure your tools go the distance is to use them only for their intended purpose. This way, they won't wear out prematurely, whether it be carbon or stainless steel. After all, nothing really lasts forever now, does it?

- **Knives and saws:** When you're dealing with trunks, roots, or branches that are too hefty for regular pliers, it's saw time dear reader. And for tidying up cuts, grafting knives are the way to go. But, here's the scoop: not all saws play by the same rules. You see, Japanese saws work their magic when you pull them towards you. So, if you're wielding one, go easy on the push or you might end up with a seriously injured blade, and the same goes for the rest of your equipment: understand how they work.

- **Pliers and shears:** When it comes to these tools, it's a real assortment! They come in every color, shape, and size to tackle all kinds of jobs—roots, branches, leaves, twigs, the whole shebang. Naturally, opt for smaller shears when you're dealing with tiny twigs and wilting flowers. Those wide standard shears? They're your go-to for thicker twigs. And if you're navigating a dense canopy, the longer shears are first prize.

- **Concave cutters:** Picture yourself as a precision surgeon wielding these cutters, crafting cuts that go deep and leave no unsightly marks. I'm talking about knob cutters, straight blades, and semi-round blades, each delivering its own special kind of cut. And don't forget, they come in different sizes, proving invaluable for gently parting branches from those cherished trunks.

- **Carving knives:** These tools are meant for working on deadwood, and they include jin pliers, chisels, loop knives, splitters, and carving hooks, just to give you an idea. Keep in mind that the aim here is to finesse your tree with minimal evidence of human touch as much as possible.

- **Repotting and roots:** When it's time to delicately extract those rootballs from your treasured pot, your trusty saws and sickle knives will come into play. You'll also want to have some angular plastic bowls for a tidy and comfortable root-working setup. And don't forget about the fantastic array of root rakes and root hooks at your disposal. They're perfect for tasks like gently combing through roots, clearing out old soil, and opening up those rootballs.

- **Trunk splitters:** This tool serves two roles: separating trunks and distinguishing live veins from the deadwood. These tasks carry some risk, so it's wise to practice on a ficus or a similar plant first. This way, you can get the hang of it before attempting it on your prized collection.

- **Wiring:** Wire is your go-to for styling, training, providing support, and making adjustments to your plant. Starting with a softer wire like aluminum, instead of copper, is a wise choice as you begin honing your bending skills. The thickness of the wire you choose should align with the size and thickness of the branch or trunk you're working on. Remember, larger and sturdier trunks call for thicker wire.

- **Protection and bending:** When you dive into the art of bending and shaping trunks and branches, it's important to safeguard your beloved plant. Rubber tubes are a nifty choice for areas with guy wires or fixation. Also, don't overlook using wet raffia or rubber tape. For added ease and safety, bring in screw clamps and sturdy steel levers to assist in your bending prows. These precautions will ensure a safer, more successful technique.

- **Maintenance:** To protect your plants from any illnesses, sanitize your instruments thoroughly. Camellia oil is excellent for keeping hinges and blades in good shape, and don't forget about the old standby, gun oil. Use grindstones and rust erasers to keep your tools shaped and sharp, as well as an assortment of brushes for a complete clean-up. And, also be sure to keep your tools dry at all times to prevent unnecessary decay.

- **Watering:** If you've got plants, a watering can is a must-have, and choosing the right watering tool ensures each bonsai receives the right amount of water, contributing to its overall health and vitality. For the bigger varieties, using a hose with a sprinkler attachment comes in really handy.

If you're looking to give your plants a light misting, you can opt for spray cans and automated watering systems are a lifesaver for keeping your plants well-hydrated. Additionally, rainwater collection from barrels or tanks with hand-operated pumps ensures soft water for sensitive species.

- **Electrical tools:** It's definitely a good move to have a diverse set of tools at your disposal. Consider looking into electrical options like the Makita, Dremel, and other rotary tools for some added efficiency when it comes to shaping, carving, and deadwood work. But, as with all power tools, proceed with caution.

- **Turntables and stands:** Turntables make life a whole lot easier when working with bigger, heavier trees. Yet again there is a wide variety available such as flat discs, ones that can tilt and are height adjustable as well. Then there are the stands for displaying the tree. Jitas, on the other hand, are small pieces of wood that are used to showcase smaller trees or other accent plants, also known as kusamono.

- **Pots:** Pots hold a pivotal role in the art of bonsai, serving both aesthetic and functional purposes. They provide the foundation for the trees, guiding their size. It's crucial to ensure that the size, style, and color of the pot complement the style and size of your bonsai, to create a harmonious balance.

Additionally, every pot needs a suitable tray, available in various sizes and materials like unglazed pottery, plastic, or ceramic. If you're aiming to enhance humidity levels, humidity trays are the way to go. Fill them with water and position them beneath the pot to increase moisture around your tree.

- **Soil and fertilizers:** It's all about finding the right combination of aeration, drainage, and moisture retention when it comes to bonsai soil. There are three main sorts to think about. First, there's Akadama, a popular choice recognized for its superior water retention and root development. Then there's Kanuma, which is great for acid-loving trees like azaleas and has excellent drainage. Finally, there's Pumice, a volcanic rock that provides excellent aeration while keeping roots from becoming saturated.

Many enthusiasts make their own blends by combining these or adding other ingredients such as lava rock or organic stuff. The objective is to select the combination that best meets your tree's demands for optimal health and growth. You will never fall short of options when it comes to fertilizers either. By choosing between chemical and organic fertilizers, you can provide your tree with the added necessary nutrients.

Now that you've got a solid grasp of the tools you'll be wielding on your bonsai adventure, let's dive into the ten essential ones you'll want in your toolkit.

2.2 Tools

As you've probably noticed, the world of bonsai offers quite a selection of tools, which could possibly leave you scratching your head. Don't worry, though. With time and practice, you'll grow more accustomed to the variety of options and their purposes.

Remember, many of the mass-produced Chinese bonsai tools labeled as "white label" often opt for more affordable alloy steel. In contrast, Japanese tools typically opt for carbon steel, known for its long-lasting sharpness.

Generally, handmade tools are like an art form in themselves. But be prepared, they can come with a pretty hefty price tag. And when I say hefty, I mean we're talking about a staggering $32,000 for a pair of meticulously crafted scissors by the master blacksmith, Yasuhiro Hirakawa.

For now, let's zoom in on the ten basic tools you'll come across in any bonsai enthusiast's kit, and we'll throw in some examples to highlight price variations.

- **Scissors:** Coming in small, medium, and large sizes, scissors are used for shaping and pruning leaves, twigs, and branches.
    - Kikuwa 200mm bonsai scissors - $23.92
    - Kamoshita gardening scissors bonsai and flower Ueki-Basami special steel blade - $275.54

- **Branch/concave cutters:** These cutters come in handy for trimming twigs and branches without leaving evident scars. They also enable more organic-looking cuts and can handle larger, thicker branches compared to bonsai scissors.
    - Wazakura hand-forged bonsai concave branch cutter 8"(200mm) - $45.99
    - Kiyozuru 102 bonsai concave cutter - $96.00

- **Knob cutters:** These cutters are employed to eliminate hefty knobs or to trim thick branches, eliminating damage to the surrounding bark. They also facilitate a smooth healing process for the cut callus.
    - Knob cutter 210mm by Matsu Bonsai Tools - $40.65
    - Bonsai knob cutter by Yoshiaki Tools 8.25" - $85.00

- **Wire cutters:** As the name implies, these cutters are designed for snipping wire. They come in various sizes to handle different wire thicknesses and offer two style variations: scissor type and bullnose.
    - Wire cutter 180mm by Matsu Bonsai Tools - $32.09
    - Hananomai stainless steel wire cutter 200mm - $105.95

- **Root cutters:** The go-to tools for trimming and training roots. Root scissors or for training and maintaining roots. On the other hand, Root Cutters are specially crafted for dealing with those hefty tap roots, making their removal a breeze.
    - Koyo masters grade stainless root cutters 7" - $135.00
    - Bonsai root cutters by Roshi Tools 8.25" (210 mm) - $36.00

- **Rakes:** Typically employed to clear out old organic fertilizer, compacted soil, and moss, these tools also come in a range of shapes and sizes. You'll find options like fine-toothed, flat, or pointed varieties to suit your specific needs.

    - Bonsai aesthetics stainless 3-prong root rake - $7.45
    - Bonsai aesthetics 2-prong root rake - $6.45

- **Tweezers:** Tweezers come in handy for delicate tasks like weeding and needle plucking on pines, a valuable tool for making those fine adjustments.

    - Stainless straight tweezers by Koyo - $9.95
    - Bonsai stainless tweezers arrow style length 170 mm/weight 145g - $27.04

- **Jin pliers:** Initially created for the task of crushing bark to create jin or deadwood, jin pliers have found additional use in bending and molding wire and branches. You can find them in small, medium, and large sizes to suit your needs.

    - Long reach bent head stainless Jin pliers by Roshi Tools 9" - $62.00
    - Koyo Masters grade stainless Jin pliers - $175.00

- **Carving tools:** These tools serve to introduce texture to both branches and the trunk, while also being handy for carving at knobs and deadwood.

    - Roshi stainless steel bonsai carving set - 5 piece - $75.00
    - Ryuga carving tool set - 6 piece - $89.95

- **Sickle:** Used for repotting to free up roots from the wall of the pot to make it easier and safer to remove the tree.

    - Bonsai transplanting sickle by Koyo Quality Tools - $11.95
    - KaKUrI sod sickle small and short sickle garden tool 7.5 Inch - $44

Alternatively, bonsai beginner starter sets are handy toolkits as well. What's neat about them is that they come in all sorts of variations, kind of like "build-your-own-pizza," but just for tools! You see, every bonsai enthusiast has their own unique style and preferences, and these kits cater to various beginner requirements. You've got sets with shears, concave cutters, tweezers, and even special brushes for grooming. It's like having your own perfect little arsenal to start your bonsai journey.

The real advantage of snagging a starter set like this is that it takes out all the guesswork. I mean, let's face it, when you're just starting out, the sheer number of tools out there is rather overwhelming. With a beginner set, you're not left scratching your head wondering, They're often curated by experienced bonsai enthusiasts who know exactly what you'll need to get started on the right foot. It's like getting a head start on your bonsai adventure. Besides, you can always purchase additional extras as needed to further expand your set.

2.2.1 Tool Care and Maintenance

Now, let's zero in on a crucial aspect that you shouldn't underestimate: Taking care of and maintaining your tools. We've given it a quick mention earlier, but it's undoubtedly worth diving into with a lot more detail.

Looking after your tools goes way beyond just having them neatly arranged and looking good. Proper care and maintenance form an integral part of your tool's longevity as well as its performance. After all, using worn-out tools can lead to harm or even the demise of your beloved trees. Let's run through a few handy tips!

- **Clean after every use:** Always make sure to clean and thoroughly dry your tools after each use. This way, you'll get rid of any dirt, sap, or debris.

- **Avoid moisture:** Always ensure your tools are thoroughly dried and completely free of any moisture. This is a major factor in preventing rust, which can be really detrimental to the tools. If you're using high-carbon steel tools, a smart move is to apply camellia oil to keep that rust away.

- **Storage:** Your tools should be kept in a dry place, preferably their own separate toolbox to further prevent rust and other damage.

- **Regular maintenance:** This will include making sure to sharpen your tools routinely to ensure that they do their job properly. Stainless steel tools will need a little more attention in the sharpening department compared to high-quality carbon steel tools. Here is a big warning: Never ever put any diamond-based sharpening tools close to your bonsai tools as these are created to remove large amounts of steel from heavy-duty tools such as axes. Steer clear, and only make use of a natural wet stone because bonsai tools are much more refined and only need very minimal material removed to be in tip-top shape.

- **Moving parts:** Give the moving parts of your tools a good oiling to keep them working smoothly and in top-notch condition. This simple step will also act as a barrier against rust.

- **Use the tools for what they're intended:** Make sure you're using the right tools for the job to avoid any unnecessary harm, not only to your tools but also to your treasured trees. And remember, these tools are meant solely for your trees—no repurposing them as nail clippers or paper scissors!

- **Avoid damaged tools:** If your tools are showing signs of rust, bending, or any other damage, it's time to consider replacing them. Using compromised tools can be risky for your tree. Consider this: a surgeon wouldn't use faulty tools on a patient, and the same goes for your trees.

2.3 Pots

In the fascinating world of bonsai, every element plays an important role when it comes to shaping your masterpiece. Pots and trays are both functional vessels and artistic canvases, enhancing the overall aesthetic. They come in various sizes, styles, and materials, each contributing to the unique charm of the miniature tree.

2.3.1 Pots

Choosing the right bonsai pot is just like picking a beautiful frame for a work of art. It's an art in itself, and believe it or not, your tree's gender is a good starting point. Take a good look at its features. If it's got graceful curves, smooth bark, and airy branches, it's leaning toward the feminine. On the contrary, thick trunks, deadwood, and sturdy branches are indicative of a more masculine tree.

Size also matters in the realm of pots. The pot should be about one-third the height of the tree, with enough room for the roots to expand comfortably. Then there's the design aspect. Unglazed pottery gives off that charming rustic charm, while glazed ceramics bring a more sophisticated feel. Make sure the colors and textures marry up with the tree's leaves and bark, weaving a unified visual story.

Pots aren't just about looks, they also have their own subtle energy. Masculine ones are rugged, with sharp lines and earthy tones, perfect for those robust trees. Feminine pots, on the other hand, boast softer lines, and intricate details, also generally adorned with lighter colors. They're the ideal match for showcasing the delicate beauty of deciduous trees.

In the end, the right pot doesn't just house your bonsai, it forms part of the artistic story.

- **Traditional Unglazed Pottery:**
    - Crafted from natural clay
    - Complements a natural aesthetic
    - Porous, promoting healthy root systems
    - Better aeration and moisture regulation

- **Glazed Ceramic Pots**:
    - The glaze provides a protective layer
    - Durable and resistant to weathering
    - A wide spectrum of vibrant colors and finishes
- **Plastic Pots**:
    - Lightweight and durable
    - Great for beginners and enthusiasts on a budget
    - A wide spectrum of vibrant colors and sizes
    - Practical and easy to maintain
- **Wooden Pots**:
    - Crafted from wood such as cedar or pine
    - Rustic charm
    - Excellent insulation - protects the roots from extreme temperatures

2.3.2 Trays

Selecting the perfect bonsai tray is all about finding that balance between form and function. The size should be slightly larger than the pot, offering a subtle frame. Material matters too. Plastic trays are lightweight and simple to clean, whilst ceramic trays radiate a classic beauty. The color should always complement the pot and tree, contributing to the harmonious visual balance. Additionally, ensure the depth of the tray can accommodate a layer of gravel for added humidity. A well-chosen tray doesn't just support, it also enhances the overall allure.

- **Humidity Trays**:
    - Shallow trays designed to hold water beneath the pot
    - Creates a microclimate for increased humidity
    - Reduces the negative impacts of dry indoor settings
    - Beneficial for species that thrive in humid conditions

- **Training and Repotting Trays**:
    - Deeper, more substantial trays
    - Employed during the repotting process
    - Provide a contained workspace
    - Prevents mess and ensures a smooth repotting process
- **Accent Plant Trays/Kusamono**:
    - Smaller trays, often intricately designed
    - Used to showcase companion plants or accent pieces
    - Serve as a stage for artistic expression
    - Allows for captivating compositions

2.4 Soil

Alright, let's take a closer look at soil. Organic soil, with components such as compost and bark, brings in those much-needed nutrients. However, it tends to get compact over time, messing with air and water flow, and potentially causing root trouble. On the contrary, inorganic soil, made up of components such as pumice and lava rock, keeps things well-ventilated and draining smoothly.

Now, the trick is, finding the right balance. Organics feed the tree, while inorganics give it structure. Think of it like this—drainage stops roots from drowning, aeration makes sure they can breathe, and water retention keeps them from getting too thirsty. It's all about the perfect juggling act to keep your bonsai thriving.

- **Akadama**: This Japanese clay soil is a popular choice due to its excellent drainage properties. It retains moisture while allowing roots to breathe, making it suitable for a wide range of tree species.
- **Pumice**:
    - Lightweight
    - Highly porous
    - Commonly used in bonsai soil mixes
    - Promotes good drainage and aeration

- **Kanuma**:
    - Acidic
    - Porous
    - Well-suited for acid-loving plants like rhododendrons
    - Aids in aeration
- **Lava Rock**:
    - Porous
    - Lightweight
    - Aids in drainage
- **Gravel**:
    - Aids in drainage
    - Helps stabilize the tree
- **Sphagnum Moss**:
    - Retains moisture
    - Used for air layering
    - Used as a top dressing in soil mixes
- **Peat Moss**:
    - Acidic
    - Moisture-retentive
    - Suitable for plants that thrive in acidic conditions.
- **Pine Bark**:
    - Aids in drainage
    - Provides structure to the soil
    - Used in soil mixes

- **Perlite**:
    - Lightweight volcanic glass
    - Helps improve aeration
- **Coconut Coir**:
    - Natural fiber extracted from coconut husks
    - Retains moisture
    - Provides aeration

2.4.1 Choosing the Right Soil

- **Consider the tree species:** Different species have different soil preferences. Thus do thorough research on the specific requirements for your species.
- **Drainage requirements:** Trees like succulents require fast-draining soils, while others may tolerate moisture retention.
- **Climate considerations:** Consider your local climate. In arid environments, moisture-retentive soil may be preferable. In humid environments, well-draining soil is crucial to prevent root rot.
- **Monitor growth and adjust:** Keep an eye on how your bonsai tree responds to the soil. Adjust the mix if you notice any signs of stress or poor growth.
- **Aeration needs:** Some trees, particularly those with fine feeder roots, benefit from well-aerated soil, thus consider soil components such as pumice or perlite.
- **PH levels:** Certain trees thrive in acidic soils, while others prefer more neutral pH levels. Choose soil components like peat moss carefully for the perfect balance.
- **Pre-packaged mixes vs. custom blends:** Pre-packaged bonsai soil mixes are convenient, but creating a custom blend allows for more precise control over your tree's soil composition.

2.5 Fertilizer

Oh yes this one needs its own little section because fertilizing is a crucial aspect of bonsai care, providing the essential nutrients that enable your miniature tree to thrive and maintain its aesthetic appeal. Thus, understanding the basics of bonsai fertilizer is very important for ensuring the health and vitality of your cherished plants. Here we'll delve into some fundamental components, selecting the right fertilizer, timing, as well as application methods to help you best navigate the aspect of nutrition for your bonsai.

2.5.1 Choosing Fertilizer

Choosing the right fertilizer is essential for providing your bonsai with the tailored nutrients it needs. Let's look at some key considerations.

- **Bonsai-specific fertilizers:** Specially formulated to meet the unique requirements of bonsai trees, these fertilizers often have balanced N-P-K ratios and may include essential micro-nutrients.

- **Liquid vs. solid fertilizers:** Solid or granular fertilizers release nutrients more gradually, providing longer-lasting benefits. On the other hand, liquid fertilizers are quickly absorbed by the roots, making them ideal for immediate nutrient uptake.

- **Organic vs. inorganic:** Organic fertilizers release nutrients gradually over time, promoting gradual and steady growth. Inorganic or chemical fertilizers offer a more immediate nutrient boost, almost like a steroid, to the plant, which is extremely beneficial during periods of rapid growth or recovery.

2.5.2 Basic Components

Fertilizer primarily consists of three key elements, often referred to as N-P-K, Each serving a distinct purpose in supporting the overall health and growth of your bonsai.

- **Nitrogen (N):** Important for foliage development and the overall growth of the plant, promoting lush, and green leaves and helping in photosynthesis.

- **Phosphorus (P):** Crucial for strong root development, as well as flower and fruit production, it also aids in the energy transfer within the plant.

- **Potassium (K):** Essential for overall vigor and resilience. It strengthens the plant's immune system, making it more resistant to diseases and other environmental stressors.

These three elements are the foundation of any good bonsai fertilizer. However, bonsai-specific fertilizers often contain a balanced ratio of N-P-K, tailored to the specific requirements of these miniature trees.

2.5.3 When to Fertilize

It's generally recommended to follow a regular feeding schedule during the growing season, which typically spans from early spring to late summer, thus timing is important when it comes to fertilizers. You will notice that timing is an aspect that tends to take center stage when it comes to bonsai cultivation.

- **Summer:** During the peak growing season, your bonsai will greatly benefit from regular fertilizer feedings. Depending on the fertilizer mix, this may range from bi-weekly or monthly.

- **Late summer to early fall:** As the days begin to shorten and growth slows down, the frequency of fertilization should be gradually decreased, helping to prepare the tree for winter dormancy.

- **Early spring:** As the bonsai emerges from dormancy and the buds start to swell, your tree will be hungry for nutrients to support the new growth.

2.5.4 How Much to Use

Dosage entirely depends on the type you're using, as well as the specific species' needs. Best to always follow the manufacturer's instructions for application rates in this regard. Generally, with solid or granular fertilizers, the standard guideline is to use a small amount sprinkled evenly over the soil surface. Liquid fertilizers should be diluted with water according to the instructions and then applied directly to the soil.

Understanding these basic components of fertilizer, and selecting the right type, timing, and application methods will empower you to appropriately nurture your bonsai and add to its longevity. Remember, each bonsai is unique, so keep a close eye on its growth patterns and adjust your fertilization routine accordingly. It's not a one-size-fits-all scenario in the wonderful world of bonsai!

2.6 Tree

Remember that buying a bonsai is a long-term investment. Take your time, do thorough research, and choose a tree that resonates with you and blends perfectly into your chosen environment, whether it be indoors or outdoors. Let's take a look at some significant factors to consider.

- **What's the purpose:** Deciding whether you want an indoor or outdoor bonsai will significantly influence your choice.

- **Your expertise level:** Beginners should opt for hardier, forgiving species that leave more room for minor mistakes in care.

- **Climate consideration:** Choose a bonsai species that is well-suited to your local climate conditions, especially if kept outdoors.

- **Available light:** Ensure you have an appropriate location with the right amount of sunlight for your species.

- **Decide on a style:** Is it going to be a formal upright, informal upright, or cascading? Choose a tree that aligns with your vision.

- **Suitability:** Learn about the species you're interested in to get a better understanding of their requirements.

- **Age consideration:** Decide whether you want to start with a young, pre-bonsai tree that you can shape from the beginning, or if you prefer a more established bonsai that requires ongoing maintenance.

- **Examine tree health:** Healthy leaves, well-distributed branches, and a balanced root system are indicators of a thriving bonsai. Keep an eye out for signs of pests, diseases, or stress.

- **Branch structure:** Ensure the branches are well-distributed, with no overcrowding or crossing.

- **Evaluate the Surface Roots/Nebari:** Look for roots that radiate evenly from the trunk. A well-developed nebari contributes to the overall aesthetic appeal of the bonsai.

- **Examine the trunk:** Thickness, taper, and movement of the trunk are all important factors that play a crucial role in the overall design and style of the tree.

- **Don't rush:** Take your time before making your final decision to be sure your tree perfectly resonates and seamlessly integrates into your environment.

- **Advice:** Consult experienced bonsai enthusiasts, local nurseries, or bonsai clubs for some expert advice. They can provide valuable insights and recommend suitable species for your location.

2.6.1 *Tree Varieties*

Ah, the spice of life, variety. Here is a list of bonsai varieties, providing a brief overview of each species, and suggestions regarding their ideal growing conditions - whether they thrive indoors, outdoors, or in both environments. This compilation aims to offer you a diverse overview of options to choose from, allowing you to select the perfect bonsai species that aligns with your preferences and capabilities.

- **Adenium obesum:** A tropical succulent that thrives indoors and is also known as the Desert Rose. It features striking, bulbous trunks and vibrant, trumpet-shaped flowers.

    o Environment: Indoors

- **Australia umbrella tree/Schefflera actinophylla:** This species is recognized for its umbrella-like canopy and glossy, compound leaves.

- Environment: Indoors

- **Bald cypress/Taxodium distichum:** A deciduous conifer, unique in the world of bonsai due to its distinctive characteristics, known for feathery foliage and distinctive fluted trunks.

    - Environment: Outdoors

- **Banyan/Ficus benghalensis:** Characterized by its aerial roots and broad canopy, the Banyan tree, a favorite for indoor bonsai enthusiasts, embodies a sense of ancient wisdom.

    - Environment: Indoors

- **Blue Jacaranda/Jacaranda mimosifolia:** This deciduous tree offers a beautiful display in outdoor bonsai gardens due to its prized vibrant blue-purple flowers.

    - Environment: Outdoors

- **Boxwood/Buxus microphylla:** Popular for formal bonsai designs, with its dense foliage and small leaves, the Boxwood is suitable for both indoor and outdoor bonsai styles.

    - Environment: Both

- **Cape jasmine/Gardenia jasminoides:** Favored for its ornamental beauty and recognizable by its waxy, white, fragrant flowers, the Cape jasmine makes an excellent indoor bonsai.

    - Environment: Indoors

- **Chinese sweet plum/Sageretia theezans:** With small, serrated leaves and delicate white flowers, the Chinese sweet plum is a favored indoor bonsai choice, and is cherished for its graceful appearance.

    - Environment: Indoors

- **Chinese elm/Ulmus parvifolia:** A popular choice among bonsai enthusiasts, it has small, serrated leaves and distinctive bark. It adapts well to both indoor and outdoor environments.

    - Environment: Both

- **Chinese wisteria/Wisteria sinensis:** Known for its cascading clusters of fragrant flowers, the Chinese wisteria is a stunning choice for outdoor enthusiasts.

    - Environment: Outdoors

- **Cissus antarctica:** It offers a unique, trailing appearance with its glossy, serrated leaves, Cissus antarctica is a vine-like species suitable for indoor bonsai cultivation.

    o   Environment: Indoors

- **Douglas fir/Pseudotsuga menziesii:** A coniferous tree with distinct needle-like leaves, the Douglas fir is a classic choice for outdoor bonsai. It exudes a sense of natural elegance.

    o   Environment: Outdoors

- **Eastern red cedar/Juniperus virginiana:** Known for its blue-green foliage and rugged bark, the Eastern red cedar is a hardy evergreen suitable for outdoor gardens.

    o   Environment: Outdoors

- **English Yew/Taxus baccata:** Offering a timeless beauty with its dark green foliage and red berries, the English Yew is a traditional choice for outdoor bonsai.

    o   Environment: Outdoors

- **European ash/Fraxinus excelsior:** With compound leaves and a rugged bark, the European ash is a resilient choice for outdoor bonsai. It imparts a sense of strength and character.

    o   Environment: Outdoors

- **European hornbeam/Carpinus betulus:** Characterized by its serrated leaves and smooth, gray bark, it offers a refined, classic look. The European hornbeam is favored for outdoor bonsai styles.

    o   Environment: Outdoors

- **Field maple/Acer campestre:** Recognized for its lobed leaves and compact growth habit, the Field maple is well-suited for outdoor bonsai enthusiasts. It offers a naturalistic appearance.

    o   Environment: Outdoors

- **Ficus microcarpa:** Known as the Chinese banyan, it features aerial roots and glossy leaves and it's a favored choice for indoor bonsai cultivation due to its adaptability.

    o   Environment: Indoors

- **Ficus retusa:** Also known as the Cuban laurel, it has small, dark green leaves. It can be grown both indoors and outdoors, making it a versatile choice for bonsai.
    - Environment: Both
- **Fukien tea tree/Carmona microphylla:** Recognized for its small, dark green leaves and tiny white flowers, the Fukien tea tree is a popular choice for indoor bonsai. It's cherished for its delicate beauty.
    - Environment: Indoors
- **Ginkgo/Ginkgo biloba:** The Ginkgo tree is known for its unique fan-shaped leaves and ancient lineage, and it exudes a sense of timelessness.
    - Environment: Outdoors
- **Hong Kong kumquat/Fortunella hindsii:** Recognized for its small, citrus fruits and glossy leaves, the Hong Kong kumquat is a favored choice for outdoor bonsai enthusiasts.
    - Environment: Outdoors
- **Jabuticaba/Plinia cauliflora:** It offers a fascinating display due to its trunk bearing fruit directly on the bark, the Jabuticaba is a unique and exotic choice for outdoor bonsai.
    - Environment: Outdoors
- **Jade plant/Crassula ovata:** Recognized for its fleshy, oval leaves and resilient nature, the Jade plant is a popular choice for indoor bonsai. It's cherished for its distinctive appearance.
    - Environment: Indoors
- **Juniperus chinensis:** Junipers are known for their rugged appearance and needle-like foliage. They are versatile and can thrive in both indoor and outdoor environments.
    - Environment: Both
- **Juniperus procumbens:** With prostrate growth and dense foliage, Juniperus procumbens offers a timeless, naturalistic appearance and is a classic choice for outdoor bonsai gardens.
    - Environment: Outdoors
- **Orange jessamine/Murraya paniculata:** Recognized for its fragrant white flowers, It exudes a sense of elegance. The Orange jessamine is a favored choice for outdoor bonsai enthusiasts.

- Environment: Outdoors

- **Pinus parviflora:** Known as the Japanese white pine, it features needle-like leaves and distinctive, textured bark. It is a versatile choice that can thrive both indoors and outdoors.

  - Environment: Both

- **Pinus thunbergii:** Also known as the Japanese black pine, it's recognized for its long, dark needles and rugged appearance.

  - Environment: Both

- **Podocarpus macrophyllus:** With small, leathery leaves, the Podocarpus offers a classic, refined appearance and is versatile. It can be grown both indoors and outdoors.

  - Environment: Both

- **Polyscias fruticosa:** Recognizable for its compound leaves, it offers a unique, tropical appearance. The Polyscias fruticosa is a favored choice for indoor bonsai enthusiasts.

  - Environment: Indoors

- **Pomegranate/Punica granatum:** Known for its vibrant, red fruits and glossy leaves, the Pomegranate tree offers a touch of natural beauty, and is a popular choice for outdoor bonsai gardens.

  - Environment: Outdoors

- **Portulacaria afra:** Recognized for its small, succulent leaves, it offers a distinctive, water-wise appearance, and is celebrated for its adaptability.

  - Environment: Both

- **Red maple/Acer rubrum:** Known for its brilliant autumn foliage, the Red maple is a classic choice for outdoor bonsai, offering a seasonal display of vibrant color.

  - Environment: Outdoors

- **Snow Rose/Serissa foetida:** A favored choice for indoor bonsai enthusiasts due to its delicate appearance with small, glossy leaves and dainty white flowers.

  - Environment: Indoors

- **Star magnolia/Magnolia stellata:** Recognized for its star-shaped, fragrant blossoms, the Star magnolia is a beautiful choice for outdoor bonsai enthusiasts, offering a touch of natural elegance.

    o   Environment: Outdoors

- **Strawberry tree/Arbutus unedo:** With distinctive, strawberry-like fruits and evergreen leaves, the Strawberry tree is a favored choice for outdoor bonsai with its unique ornamental display.

    o   Environment: Outdoors

- **Sycamore maple/Acer pseudoplatanus:** Known for its lobed leaves and rugged bark, the Sycamore maple is a classic choice for outdoor bonsai, exuding a sense of natural elegance.

    o   Environment: Outdoors

- **Ulmus minor:** Recognizable for its serrated leaves and distinctive bark, Ulmus offers a timeless, classic appearance.

    o   Environment: Outdoors

- **Vine maple/Acer circinatum:** Offering a seasonal display of natural beauty, the Vine maple is a favored choice for outdoor bonsai enthusiasts with its lobed leaves and striking autumn colors.

    o   Environment: Outdoors

- **Virginia pine/Pinus virginiana:** Known for its rugged appearance and needle-like foliage, the Virginia pine imparts a sense of strength and character.

    o   Environment: Outdoors

Keep in mind that choosing a bonsai is almost like adopting a new family member. Every tree has its own special personality and story. With some thoughtful attention and TLC, your bonsai will grow into a treasured living masterpiece.

And don't forget, having the right tools and knowing how to use them, plus giving them the care they deserve, is key to making your bonsai journey a success.

3
Preparation

Are you aiming for a wild, natural look or a more refined, structured appearance? You have to think about this. First off, preparation sets the stage for your bonsai journey. It helps you envision the end result and better plan out the steps to attain it. Understanding your goal will set the tone for everything else including preparation. Remember, all these steps tie together to create the perfect environment for your bonsai to thrive. Goal setting guides your journey, soil pH keeps your tree happy and healthy, and proper illumination gives it the energetic boost it needs to grow strong and vibrant. It's like giving your bonsai the VIP treatment!

We are going to dive into preparing the perfect spot for your tree, so without further ado, let's get started.

3.1 Soil

Yes, we are back at soil again, and with good reason because soil is probably one of the aspects of the whole process that you have the most control over. Getting a firm understanding of your chosen species' soil preferences and getting it all set up in advance is a smart move.

Considering bonsais have a very limited space to grow, it's important to set up the perfect soil environment for your tree to thrive. Now, when you purchase a tree, the existing soil mix is pretty much a guessing game. Whether it's a pre-potted tree or you're doing some repotting, you've got to get rid of as much of that old soil from the roots as possible. There's no negotiating this fact. That means taking the plant out of its container and giving it a fresh start. But, be gentle.

Knowing your tree's preferences ensures it's getting the right nutrients, and mixing your own allows for much more control. This way, you can fine-tune the environment to suit your plant's specific needs. However, might I add that ready-made substrates are a handy invention?

Let's talk about soil pH.

3.1.1 Soil PH

It might sound a bit technical when you delve into it, but it's actually a big deal for your bonsai's well-being. Different tree species thrive at different pH levels.

Gather a bunch of bonsai enthusiasts and throw in the word "soil," and you will be entertained for hours with varying opinions and perspectives. There are all sorts, the high rollers importing stuff from Japan right through to the mavericks using cat litter. However, central to this debate, the fact remains that soil pH levels are a delicate dance. Understanding and managing soil acidity is not just a skill, but an art form that can significantly impact the health and vitality of your tree.

Before we delve into the nuanced world of soil pH for bonsais, let's unravel the concept of the pH scale itself. This scale is a measure of the acidity or alkalinity of a substance, ranging from 0 to 14. A pH of 7 is neutral, indicating a perfect balance between acid and alkaline properties. Anything below 7 is acidic, while anything above 7 is alkaline. Simple, right? Different species have distinct preferences when it comes to soil pH. Understanding these specific needs is like speaking the language of your tree. For instance, acid-loving species will thrive in soil with a lower pH, which is generally around 4.5 to 6.5. On the other hand, species that thrive in a more alkaline environment, clocks in with a pH range of 6.5 to 7.5.

3.1.2 Finding the Balance

While each species has its preferred pH range, there exists a universal spot that in general works well for a wide variety of bonsai species. This would be mildly acidic to slightly alkaline soil with a pH of 6 to 7. This range provides a versatile foundation, accommodating various species' diverse preferences. Your bonsai communicates through its leaves, branches, and soil.

Observing these cues is critical in determining if your tree is content with its pH levels. Yellowing leaves, stunted growth, or a decline in overall vigor can be strong indicators of a pH mismatch. Best to get yourself a pH testing kit as part of your prep set. Regular checks of your soil's pH levels will help you fine-tune these little nuances to provide your tree with the perfect environment.

3.1.3 The Art of Modification

Modifying soil pH is a fine art, best you approach it with caution and precision. To lower pH levels (increase acidity) for acid-loving species, organic materials like sphagnum moss or pine bark can be introduced into the soil mixture. For alkaline-loving trees, additions such as agricultural lime can help elevate pH levels. Managing soil pH is a valuable skill in cultivation, it's essential to remember that abrupt and drastic changes can be detrimental. Thus, always be sure to introduce modifications gradually, allowing the tree enough time to adapt to the changes. Even though trees are remarkably resilient, they do require a gentle touch and some insight into their preferences.

By deciphering the language of acidity and alkalinity, you can unleash the full potential of your miniature piece of nature. With patience, observation, and a touch of artistry, you can find the perfect balance where the pH forms a strong cornerstone of success.

3.2 Pot

To get your container ready, start by covering up any drainage holes with a screen. It's a bit like giving your tree a comfy mattress to grow on. Except that this mattress ensures proper drainage to prevent root rot. Never skip this step.

You can either grab a pre-made metal or plastic screen. Alternatively, a lot of people opt for a simple window screen cut to size. Simply lay down the screen over the drainage holes and cover it with an evenly spread thin layer of your soil mixture. This will form the foundation for your bonsai which provides a stable base for the roots to settle into.

3.3 Light

Bonsais need their daily dose of sunshine. After all, it's their main source of energy! I will say it again, when it comes to nurturing a bonsai, understanding its natural habitat is key. Let's look at some insights that will enable you to pick the perfect spot.

If you're keeping your bonsai indoors, make sure it gets plenty of natural light. For those starting out with bonsai, it's worth noting that some beginner-friendly species are well-suited for indoor cultivation. Jade, Ficus, and Jasmine are some good candidates. If you're going for an outdoor setup, find a spot where it can soak up those sun rays without getting burnt. Yet again, light requirements are all species-dependent, however, they all need either full- or partial sun. Whether indoors or outdoors you will need to assess the space and keep an eye on the amount of light it receives throughout the day. Another factor is the light intensity. Some species love bright direct light while others prefer more filtered, indirect light.

Let's talk about light direction for a moment. Depending on where you're situated in our beautiful world, south-facing windows usually get the lion's share of sunlight during the day. North-facing ones, on the other hand, offer up a softer, indirect glow. East and west-facing windows strike a nice balance between the two. Let's throw some seasonal changes into the mix. Summers bring longer, more intense sunlight, while winters bring shorter, milder rays. You'll have to shuffle your bonsai's position accordingly.

Don't forget about the magic of LED or fluorescent grow lights. They can step in and supplement natural light to give your bonsai the light it needs to flourish. With these lights, you can also create a more controlled lighting environment for your tree. Last but not least, keep a close watch for any signs of sunburn on your tree. If you spot withering or discoloration, it might be time to rethink the location. A good tip is to give your bonsai a little turn every now and then to ensure all sides get a fair share of light.

3.4 Temperature

Life's not just about soil, pruning, and watering schedules when it comes to the world of bonsai. Navigating the temperature of the environment beforehand and throughout is important. And interestingly enough, temperature is one of the most overlooked aspects.

Alright, let's talk about preparing and creating the perfect climate for your bonsai. This is absolutely crucial for its overall well-being. Think of it as finding your tree's comfort zone. Some trees love it warm, while others are hardier and can handle the cold. That's why understanding your local hardiness zone is yet another important aspect. It provides crucial information about the average minimum winter temperatures in your region, helping you pick bonsai species that are just right for your climate.

Now, when winter rolls around, it's highly advisable to have a game plan in check. For species that aren't as hardy, frost can be a real problem. It can harm those delicate leaves and branches, at times even irreversibly. So, best to be ready with alternatives. Consider bringing your bonsai indoors or finding a sheltered spot, like a garage or porch. Some folks even go the extra mile by burying their trees, leaving just the top branches peeking out. A layer of snow up to the first branches can also provide some much-needed extra insulation.

Summer has its challenges too, as you are aware of by now. Sunburn, dehydration, and even root rot are all things to watch out for. Make sure you've got cooler, shaded spots in your environment where your bonsai can seek refuge. Then there is the hunt you will have to embark on for a little gem known as microclimates. In any garden, you'll discover microclimates which are small areas with their own unique temperature characteristics. These little nooks can have their own unique temperature quirks and can be warmer or cooler than the surrounding area, providing you with opportunities to grow a wider range of species.

Monitoring tools such as something as basic as a thermometer will undoubtedly be worth your while. They help you keep a close eye on temperature fluctuations, allowing you to make timely adjustments to protect your bonsai. So, make sure it's on your prep list.

Ultimately, understanding your bonsai's needs and its natural rhythm includes informed temperature care, ensuring it thrives in its own little world.

3.5 Tool Maintenance Material

Taking care of your bonsai tools is more than just a chore, it forms a fundamental part of ensuring your bonsai endeavor runs as seamlessly as possible. To keep your tools in prime condition, you'll want to have a few essential items on hand. Let's have a rundown of some must-have materials to stock up on that will keep your bonsai tools performing their best.

- **Boiled linseed oil:** A common choice for tool maintenance, boiled linseed oil penetrates metal surfaces, providing protection against rust. It's easy to apply and dries to a protective finish.

- **Camellia oil:** This natural oil is renowned for its rust-prevention properties. Applying a thin coat of camellia oil after each use forms a protective barrier that guards against moisture and oxidation.

- **Fine-grit sandpaper/sharpening stones:** Used for honing and sharpening the edges of your tools. Fine grit sandpaper (around 400-600 grit) or dedicated sharpening stones are essential for maintaining a sharp cutting edge.

- **Cloth rags:** Soft, clean cloth rags are handy for applying oils and cleaning tools. They help ensure an even distribution of protective coatings.

- **Brass brush:** A brass brush is useful for removing stubborn sap, resin, or other residues from your tools. Its bristles are strong enough to clean without scratching the metal surface.

3.6 Understand Your Calendar

To truly nurture and cultivate these miniature marvels, you have to become attuned to the rhythm of the seasons and the unique needs of each species during each of these seasons. This seasonal awareness empowers you to anticipate and best plan for potential changes. We will delve into the nuanced yet significant transitions that govern a tree's development throughout the year.

3.6.1 Winter Dormancy

The year begins with the hibernation period: winter. As the days grow shorter and the air turns crisp, the tree eases into a state of dormancy; respite, and conservation. Don't for one minute think that this phase is a time of inactivity, rather, it's a period of focused energy conservation.

Intercession:

- **Reduce watering:** Carefully monitor soil moisture to avoid overwatering because of the slowed metabolic rate the bonsai's water requirements diminish. Overwatering can lead to root rot.

- **Pest vigilance:** Although pests are less active in winter, you will still need to regularly inspect your bonsai for any signs of infestations.

- **Protect from frost:** Shield the bonsai from freezing temperatures by placing it in a sheltered location or utilizing protective covers as we have discussed.

Tips and Tricks:

- **Stable environment:** Maintain a consistent temperature and humidity level to provide as much of a stable environment as possible for your dormant miniature tree.

- **Minimize disturbance:** Avoid any major changes and interventions such as repotting during this period to prevent unnecessary stress.

- **Pruning:** Light maintenance pruning may be conducted, focusing on removing dead or damaged branches if desired.

3.6.2 Revival and Flowering

With the arrival of spring, the bonsai awakens from its dormancy. Buds swell and unfurl into vibrant leaves, breathing fresh life into your tree. This period is marked by a surge of growth and arrays of delicate blossoms for some species.

Intercession:

- **Fertilization:** Provide a balanced, slow-release fertilizer to support the growth surge.

- **Pruning:** Trim away any excessive growth to encourage denser foliage and maintain the desired shape.

- **Repotting:** Just before new growth emerges, in early spring, consider repotting to refresh the soil and encourage healthy new root development.

- **Wiring and training:** Apply or adjust wiring to guide branches into the desired form while they are still pliable.

Tips and Tricks:

- Sun exposure: Ensure your bonsai gets ample sunlight for healthy growth, but shield it from the intense midday sun, which can lead to leaf burn.

- **Monitor watering:** Your bonsai may require more water due to increased growth, thus keep the soil consistently moist but avoid waterlogging.

- **Pest control:** Pests become more active during spring, so keep a watchful eye to take timely action when needed.

3.6.3 Producing New Growth and Fruit

Lush foliage blankets the branches, and for some species, tiny fruits begin to form as summer unfolds. This is a period of exuberance that does demand attentive care.

Intercession:

- **Regular watering:** Maintain consistent and thorough watering to ensure the soil remains evenly moist.

- **Pinching and pruning:** Pinching back new shoots and pruning overgrown areas to keep the growth in check and your tree well-maintained.

- **Disease and pest management:** Keep a watchful eye out for signs of infestation or disease. Always act promptly to prevent further spreading and damage.

Tips and Tricks:

- **Provide shade:** Shield your bonsai from the intense midday sun to prevent leaf burn. Partial shade or filtered light will be required.

- **Humidity management:** Mist the foliage, especially during hot, dry spells, to maintain humidity.

- **Fertilize strategically:** Adjust your fertilizer routine to support continued growth without going into overdrive.

3.6.4 Short Period of Summer Dormancy

In some climates, particularly those with scorching summers, bonsai trees may experience a brief period of dormancy. This serves as a natural mechanism to conserve energy and reduce stress during the hottest months.

Intercession:

- **Reduced watering:** The slowed metabolic rate of the tree will require you to adjust your watering schedule to avoid waterlogging.

- **Limit pruning:** In order to avoid any additional stress, minimize major pruning during this period.

- **Monitor health:** During summer dormancy you will still have to keep a watchful eye on your bonsai for signs of stress or pests.

3.6.5 Consolidation of New Growth

As temperatures cool and days shorten, autumn brings a breathtaking display of changing foliage. It's a season of transition, where your bonsai prepares for the dormancy of winter.

Intercession:

- **Leaf pruning:** Thin out overloaded areas to allow dappled sunlight to reach the inner branches.

- **Wiring adjustments:** Examine the wires for indications of cutting in and make the adjustments that are needed to avoid scarring.

- **Protect against frost:** As temperatures drop, shelter your tree from any cold winds and frost.

Tips and Tricks:

- **Selective leaf removal:** Promote the growth of smaller, more refined leaves by removing older leaves.

- **Adjust feeding:** Reduce fertilization to facilitate slowing down the growth pace, preparing the tree for winter dormancy.

- **Strengthening defenses:** Incorporate preventative measures and treatments against pests and pathogens before winter strikes.

3.6.6 Winter Dormancy

And so the cycle comes full circle with winter again. The bonsai, having absorbed the energy of the seasons, eases back into its resting period which is very important for its long-term health and vitality.

Intercession:

- **Reduced watering:** Your bonsai's water needs will reduce as its metabolic rate slows down. Maintain a careful balance to prevent dehydration or water pooling.

- **Protection from frost:** To safeguard your tree from the hardship of winter, provide adequate insulation and shelter.

- **Reflection and planning:** Reflect on the year's progress and plan ahead for the next cycle by identifying any changes to your care routine that could be improved.

Tips and Tricks:

- **Optimal conditions:** Make sure your bonsai is in an environment with consistent temperature and humidity.

- **Gentle pruning:** Light maintenance pruning, while optional, can be done to remove any dead or damaged branches.

- **Pest inspection:** They might be less active, but pests can still pose a threat, they always do. Thus regular inspection for any signs of infestation should always be on your checklist.

With each passing season, you will become more knowledgeable and advanced in your care routine.

3.7 Bonsai Goals

If you want to become a bonsai master, you must establish some goals that will help you expand and refine your craft. By prioritizing quality over quantity, incorporating new techniques, and consistently expanding your knowledge base, you will undoubtedly enhance your skills. It may sound like a lot, but once you immerse yourself in this journey, you'll be surprised at how quickly you adapt. Your goals will naturally evolve as your skills and knowledge grow. To kickstart your journey, let's explore a couple of different aspects of setting and achieving bonsai goals.

- **Quality, not quantity:** When it comes to bonsai, the concept of less is more rings true. Instead of collecting a mass of trees, it's wiser to invest time and effort into perfecting a few. Each tree is a living work of art that demands careful attention to detail. You may properly master the strategies and intricacies of each specific species by devoting adequate resources to the development of a select few trees.

- **Incorporate new techniques:** Mastery of bonsai calls for constant exploration and application of new techniques. Experimentation with different wiring styles, pruning methods, and soil compositions will broaden the skill set of any bonsai artist. Accepting change and adapting to new practices not only expands the artistic skill set but also builds a deeper connection with the trees.

- **Expand your knowledge:** This art form requires a profound understanding of the unique characteristics and needs of each species. Thus, it's important to embark on a journey of continuous learning where you have to study the habits, growth patterns, and specific care requirements of various trees. Having this knowledge will empower you to make informed decisions that will ensure the well-being of your trees.

- **Attend events and workshops:** Immersing yourself in the vibrant atmosphere of bonsai events and workshops is undoubtedly an enriching experience! These events provide you with access to renowned artists, expert advice, and a wide range of bonsai specimens. By participating in these workshops, you gain practical skills, refine your techniques, and build connections with fellow bonsai artists. These events offer an environment to celebrate the art form and become an active participant in a community of like-minded people.

- **Expanding your library:** Books on the art of bonsai are troves of knowledge, providing perspectives from skilled artists and horticultural professionals. By continually expanding your bonsai library, you will have constant access to a wealth of knowledge, fundamental principles, and advanced techniques. After all, continuous learning is essential in every aspect of life and it's no different when it comes to improving your talents and refining your vision in the world of bonsai.

- **Explore online forums and local clubs:** Engaging with a global community opens doors to fresh perspectives and fosters an environment of exploration and learning. Conversely, becoming a member of a local bonsai club offers a chance for a more immersive experience, mentorship, and the chance to establish a supportive network.

- **Ad a tree a year:** When it comes to bonsai, the cliché "slow and steady wins the race" most certainly rings true. Adding one tree to your collection each year offers a sustainable pace for expansion. This timely approach provides for a more in-depth understanding of each new tree, allowing you to better develop your skills and refine your awareness.

You can truly hone your craft by setting and achieving bonsai goals, prioritizing quality, adding trees mindfully, expanding species knowledge, embracing new techniques, and engaging with the bonsai community.

The bonsai journey is a lifelong endeavor characterized by continuous learning, development, and evolution. With dedication and a passion for excellence, you will unlock your potential to create a living masterpiece that will inspire you.

4
Cultivation

Cultivating bonsai is a captivating blend where nature and human creativity harmoniously merge, turning ordinary trees into living masterpieces. Now, this whole magical procedure begins with planting a young tree in a shallow pot to limit root growth and keep the tree tiny. Simple right?

The roots are then trimmed on a regular basis to keep them compact and establish fine feeder roots. Pruning is another crucial task that forms the branches and foliage pads to give the bonsai its uniquely distinctive shape. Wiring, another fun, yet crucial technique, involves gently wrapping wire around branches, you can guide their growth and create your own personal desired aesthetic. Diligent care is required for the right balance of water, light, and nutrients. Then there's the science of soil. Soil must drain well to prevent root rot and should benefit from regular feeding during the growing season. I reiterate that patience is key in the process because these trees evolve slowly, responding to your meticulous guidance over time. It's a journey of discovery and a true testament to the power of nature.

In the end, bonsai isn't merely about growing trees; it's about nurturing and sculpting a living art form over time. It's about finding calm in the focused discipline of tending to these small trees and recognizing the beauty in every twist and curve of the branches. It's an excursion that requires patience, ingenuity, and a deep appreciation for our natural world's beauty.

Let's take a closer look at some aspects when it comes to cultivating your tree.

4.1 Potting

More than just mere containers, bonsai pots play a very important role in the art of cultivation. They are a canvas that should not only serve a functional purpose by housing your tree but also complement the magnificent aesthetics of your tree, stretching beyond just form meeting function.

Remember, when picking out a pot, think about its size, shape, and color. It's crucial that the pot matches the proportions of your tree and adds to the overall visual appeal. The depth of the pot matters too; shallow ones work best for delicate branches, while deeper ones suit sturdier trunks and foliage. Let's talk about color! The pot's hue should harmonize with your tree's leaves and bark, telling a cohesive visual story. Material is another significant factor. Traditional pots are made of clay, and this allows for excellent moisture retention and aeration. On the other hand, we have glazed ceramics that have a modern, sleek appeal to them. Unglazed pots are another option that will radiate a rustic charm and evoke a lovely natural feel. Remember, the pot is a reflection of your artistic vision and a vessel for the tree's story.

4.1.1 How to Pot

- **Get your tools:** Be sure you have all the tools you will need in arms reach. You'll need a pot, a screen to cover the drainage hole, your bonsai soil, and of course, your tree!

- **Prep the pot:** First things first, and that is to cover the drainage hole at the bottom of your pot with a screen. This will prevent any precious soil from escaping while still allowing water to drain properly.

- **Add your first layer of soil:** Next up, you will put a thin layer of bonsai soil at the bottom of the pot, to provide a sturdy base for your tree's roots.

- **Remove your tree:** Here you will have to proceed with caution. Gently remove your bonsai from its current pot and keep a steady hand to not damage any of the roots.

- **Root trim:** Take a close look at the roots. If you notice any dead, diseased, or tangled parts, trim them and remove them. But, be sure not to snip and trim too much though.

- **Tree positioning:** It's all about height and position when placing your tree in the pot. Make sure that your tree is a tad bit off-center to create a more natural look.

- **Add soil:** Fill in the space around the roots with more bonsai soil, making sure to get it into all the little nooks and crannies.

- **Compact the soil:** Now you will have to eliminate any air pockets that might be around the roots. You can simply make use of a chopstick or something similar to gently press down on the soil.

- **Water:** Voila! Your tree is securely potted, and now it's time to give it a good watering that will help settle the soil and hydrate the roots.

- **Clean Up:** And just like that, you are done with potting. Be sure to give your pot a good wipe down, remove any excess soil, and give your tree a final scan for any loose debris.

- **Monitor and adjust:** You will have to keep a diligent eye on your bonsai over the next few weeks. If you notice any problems with regard to growth and leaves, it's time for troubleshooting, and you will have to reassess and repot.

4.2 Pruning

Pruning your bonsai is almost like giving it a good haircut, however, it's not just all about looks, but for its overall well-being too.

When you trim away extra branches and leaves, you are allowing your tree's energy to flow where it truly matters, to grow and flourish. You are essentially giving your tree some space to breathe by decluttering it from old debris, this also keeps any possible health issues at bay. A little trim here and there keeps it just the way you want it and maintains its fascinating miniature size. Plus, regular pruning helps your bonsai look all mature and well-maintained, giving it that polished, refined look.

4.2.1 How to Prune

- **Get your gear:** For your pruning session, gather your pruning shears, branch cutters, and a pair of gloves to protect yourself against any scratches. It's pivotal to ensure your tools are clean, as you'll be making cuts on your tree that create wounds requiring healing. Clean tools help prevent the introduction of harmful bacteria, fungi, and pests that could lead to unwanted infections and diseases.

- **Set the stage:** You will need to have some good lighting to be able to properly hone in on the details. So make sure you are in a spot that has ample light or is well-lit.

- **Plan:** Take a good look at your bonsai to properly plan what needs to get snipped and trimmed. You can just go in and start cutting, it is a fine art that does require insight and planning.

- **Start with the obvious:** The first cutting that needs to be done is to remove any dead, damaged, or diseased branches.

- **Crossing branches:** Up next is to spot any branches crossing or rubbing against each other. If you notice any crossing or rubbing, be sure to pick the stronger one, snip, and remove the other.

- **Thin out excess:** You also have to give your bonsai some room to breathe by thinning out any branches where you notice overly dense growth. Work slowly in order to avoid over-trimming.

- **Style:** Now it's time for fine-tuning, shaping, and pruning your tree according to the style you envision. As an example, for a windswept look, focus your pruning skills on one side only.

- **Evaluate:** Take a step back and inspect your tree to make a final assessment if any further pruning is required.

- **Water:** After pruning, give your tree a good watering.

4.3 Wiring and Shaping

Rome wasn't wired in a day! Wiring and shaping your bonsai is a personalized experience that's all about coaxing the branches to dance the way you want them to. But why exactly do we need to do it? Simply put, it helps guide the growth of the tree, and it adds character. Wiring essentially allows you to sculpt your own living artwork.

Now, choosing the right wire is key, and you'll want to pick a wire that's suited for your tree and your artistic vision. Aluminum wire is a popular choice, easy to work with, and comes in various thicknesses to suit different branches. For heavier, more stubborn branches, copper wire is the heavyweight champion. In general, your wire should be about a third of the branch's thickness.

But first, let's take a deeper look at how to wire and what to consider.

4.3.1 How to Wire

Choosing Wire

- **Assess the branch thickness:** To be able to make the right pick when it comes to wire gauge, you need to determine the thickness of the branches you intend to wire.

- **Make the right pick:** If you want to wire thinner branches, a lighter gauge will do the trick. And, for thicker branches, you will evidently require heavier gauge wire.

- **Consider wire material:** Is it going to be aluminum or copper wire? Aluminum is softer and easier to work with, while copper, on the other hand, provides more holding strength.

- **Wire flexibility:** Ensure the wire you choose is pliable enough and that it would be easy for you to work with.

- **Wire length:** You will have to estimate the length of wire that you will use by measuring the branch to be wired. It's always better to have a bit extra than to run short.

- **You can use multiple gauges:** You most certainly can make use of different wire gauges for various branches on the same tree. This is especially handy if they vary significantly in thickness.

- **Consider color:** You don't want your tree to look like a telephone pole, thus choose a wire color that blends well with the bark of your bonsai to make it less noticeable.

- **Quality of coating:** When it comes to wire coating that will prevent corrosion over time, anodized or annealed wires are good solutions.

- **Cost:** You get what you pay for, and high-quality wire is, unfortunately, more expensive; nonetheless, it is an investment in the health of your tree.

- **Stock up on various gauges:** Variety is the spice of life, and having a variety of wire gauges at hand is highly recommended.

- **Environmental factors:** Take into account factors like weather conditions and potential corrosion due to rain, especially if your tree is placed outdoors.

Single Wiring

- **Gather your materials:** Yes, you need to have all the necessary tools at hand: bonsai wire (appropriate gauge), wire cutters, and optionally, pliers for adjustments.

- **Pick a branch:** Simply pick the branch that you want to wire and consider its thickness and the desired shape you want to achieve.

- **The right gauge:** Now, you need to choose a wire with a gauge that matches your chosen branch. It should be strong enough to hold the branch in place without cutting into and damaging the bark.

- **Measure and cut:** Measure your branch and cut the appropriate length of wire. Remember to cut that little bit extra.

- **Anchor the wire:** Start at the base of the branch and slowly and gently spiral the wire around it. Keep wiring toward the tip of the branch and be sure the wire is snug but not overly tight.

- **Spacing:** The wire coils should be evenly spaced along the branch in order to distribute pressure evenly, allowing for more natural growth.

- **Angle:** Keep an eye on the wire's angle since it will guide the branch in the direction you want it to bend. Patience is essential to ensure flawless execution and achieve the desired results.

- **Space near the tips:** Always leave a small gap without any wire near the tip of the branch as these are delicate pieces that do not need to incur excessive pressure.

- **Secure the end:** When you reach the end of your spiral at the branch tip, simply secure the end of the wire by tucking it underneath the nearest coil.

- **Adjusting branch position:** Here you will need to proceed with caution. To adjust your branch's position, slowly and gently bend the wired branch into the shape you want. These adjustments should be made gradually to avoid any damage.

- **Monitoring growth:** You will have to monitor the wired branch over time to ensure the wire is not cutting into the bark.

Double Wiring

- **Gather your materials:** Yes, you need to have all the necessary tools at hand: bonsai wire (appropriate gauge), wire cutters, and optionally, pliers for adjustments.

- **Pick a branch:** Simply pick the branch that you want to wire and consider its thickness and the desired shape you want to achieve.

- **The right gauge:** Here you will need to select two wires of different thicknesses. The thicker wire will be your primary wire and is used to provide support. Your thinner wire will be your secondary wire which will facilitate shaping the branch.

- **Measure and cut:** Measure your branch and cut the appropriate length of wires. Cut that little bit extra.

- **Anchor your primary wire:** Yet again, you will begin at the base of the chosen branch and gently start spiraling the primary wire around it towards the tip of the branch. Be sure that the wire is snug and not overly tight.

- **Spacing:** The primary wire coils should be evenly spaced along the branch in order to distribute pressure evenly, allowing for more natural growth.

- **Anchor your secondary wire:** Start at the base again, this time with your secondary wire, spiraling it along the primary wire. Be sure to keep both wires parallel to each other.

- **Angle:** Keep an eye on the angle of both wires since it will guide the branch in the direction you want it to bend.

- **Space near the tips:** Always leave a small gap without any wire near the tip of the branch as these are delicate pieces that do not need to incur excessive pressure.

- **Secure the end:** When you reach the end of your spiral at the branch tip, simply secure the end of both wires by tucking it underneath the nearest coil.

- **Adjusting branch position:** Proceed with caution. Adjust your branch's position, by slowly and gently bending the wired branch into the shape you want. These adjustments should be made gradually to avoid any damage.

- **Monitoring growth:** You will have to monitor the wired branch over time to ensure the wire is not cutting into the bark.

Guy Wiring

Guy wiring comes in handy when you've got branches that are a bit too tough for regular wiring. The goal here is to guide them in one particular direction rather than making curves.

Now, here's the interesting part: when you coil branches, it causes trauma to the tree, and the tree responds by growing in response to the trauma. Guy wiring, on the other hand, is a smoother operation. It causes less trauma to the tree, and the bending is spread out over a longer section of the branch. So, it takes a bit more time and patience compared to the twists and turns of regular wiring.

- **Gather your materials:** Yes, you need to have all the necessary tools at hand: bonsai wire (appropriate gauge), wire cutters, and optionally, pliers for adjustments.

- **Pick a branch:** Simply pick the branch that you want to wire and consider its thickness and the desired shape you want to achieve.

- **Wrap protective material:** Wrap protective material around the branch to prevent any damage during the process.

- **Create an anchor point:** Apply a hook—you can bend a piece of wire into a "u" shape, to create an anchor point for the guy wire on the branch.

- **Attachment point:** Next, you will need to choose the attachment point for the guy wire. This can be either fixed to your pot, or even a strong surface root.

- **Connect:** Connect the anchor point of the branch with a thin wire, making sure it's secure but not too tight, avoiding damage to the branch.

- **Bend:** Slowly and gently bend your branch into the desired position.

- **Monitoring growth:** You will have to monitor the wired branch over time to ensure the wire is not cutting into the bark.

4.4 Propagation

If patience is your game, then seeds would be an enjoyable endeavor because it offers an opportunity to nurture and foster your tree from the earliest stage. Yet again, you will have to be aware of your choice of species, as some are easier to propagate from seeds compared to others. One huge positive is the fact that you can curve and shape your bonsai from a very early age.

On the other hand, when you grow a tree from cuttings, you are basically fostering new life from a sprig of the original tree. Working from cuttings requires you to take a piece from a mature tree and then sprout roots from it. This is usually done with a piece of branch or twig and does require some skill. Then, there is nursery stock, which is a young pre-grown tree. It's not exactly a blank slate such as with a seedling or cutting, but at least you can already make some form of assessment with regard to the potential of the tree.

Each propagation method has its own positives and challenges. But one thing remains certain, and that is irrespective of the route you choose when it comes to propagation, it remains a rewarding endeavor.

4.4.1 Growing From Seeds

Do you want to witness a complete lifecycle? Grow a bonsai from a seed! One thing you must understand is that there is no such thing as "special bonsai seeds." All bonsai tree seeds are simply seeds from regular trees.

Thus, if you are looking for a bonsai that will truly merge with your environment, consider seeds from trees in your surroundings. This is a surefire way to know that your tree will perfectly adapt to your environment, almost like giving it a headstart to thriving. Irrespective of where your seed is from, one thing that you will have to understand is stratification. Stratification is the process that mimics the natural conditions that seeds are subjected to in nature, being dormant in winter and germinating in early spring. Thus, if your seeds are from a different climate area or you decided to start planting out of season, you might have to simulate the cold moist winter conditions to help better prepare the seeds for germination.

Planting seeds is a fairly simple procedure, and it is no different from planting any other seeds when it comes to bonsai.

- **Choose a container:** Use a shallow tray or pot that has good drainage to prevent waterlogging.

- **Prep your soil:** A well-draining bonsai soil mixture with proper aeration and moisture retention will work wonders to get started. Add this mixture to your pot or tray.

- **Sow the seeds:** Simply evenly space your seeds on the soil surface and gently press them into the soil.

- **Add soil:** Cover the seeds with a thin layer of soil to help maintain the moisture level.

- **Indirect light:** Place your tray or pot in indirect light.

- **Watering:** Keep the soil moist by consistently misting the surface to prevent the seeds from drying out.

- **Patience is key:** Germination doesn't happen overnight, you can expect anywhere from a few weeks to several months, depending on the species.

4.4.2 Growing From Cuttings

Growing from cuttings works especially well with deciduous trees and some conifers. As previously said, some skill will be required to sprout forth a new miniature tree from the parent plant. Let's take a look at how you can get started.

- **Select the perfect branch:** Look for a healthy, young branch or twig on an existing tree of your choice. This branch will be the parent material of your new bonsai.

- **Size matters:** For the best chances of success, aim for cuttings that are between 2-4 inches in length and about 1/8 inch thick. You can use larger cuttings, however, the success rate for shooting roots is a lot less with these.

- **All about timing:** Spring and early summer are your best bets for taking cuttings. During these periods there is still active growth occurring, ensuring that the cutting is filled with the necessary nutrients and hormones for successful rooting.

- **Prepare the cuttings:** After you've chosen the branch, make a clean cut using pruning shears. Make sure that your shears are both sharp and sterile. Remove all of the unnecessary leaves and twigs from the bottom of the cutting, leaving only a few leaves on top to allow for photosynthesis.

- **Rooting hormone as an option:** While not mandatory, applying a rooting hormone can encourage quicker root development.

- **Plant the cuttings:** Fill a small pot or container with your bonsai soil mix and simply place your cuttings into the soil. Be sure that the soil is adequately watered and moist.

- **Care:** Ensure that the soil remains consistently moist but not waterlogged. Position your cutting in an area with indirect sunlight. If desired, you can create a makeshift greenhouse effect by covering it with translucent plastic, providing an additional boost for growth.

- **Patience is key:** Rooting doesn't happen overnight, you can expect anywhere from a few weeks to several months, depending on the species. Keep your eye out for any new growth and lightly tug on the cutting to test for any resistance.

4.4.3 Nursery Stock

Yet again, timing is key and when you are interested in purchasing nursery stock, early spring to late summer would be a good time to make your pick.

So what should you keep your eyes peeled for when it comes to selecting the perfect nursery stock? Firstly, kick off with a thorough examination of the trunk, ensuring it boasts a sturdy build and exhibits proper tapering. The trunk, after all, serves as the tree's backbone. Pay close attention to the tapering, seeking a gradual and majestic rise to the top. Branches are the next focal point. Their distribution is key, contributing to a harmoniously balanced structure. As for the roots, avoid excessive tangling, though some circling can be fixed later. Lastly, consider the tree's character. Look for fascinating elements like unique twists or captivating gnarls that lend it a distinctive charm.

Here you have it: a brief introduction to your cultivation journey that will set you well on your way when it comes to potting, pruning, wiring, and propagation. These are all fundamental practices that form the foundation of nurturing your living piece of art. Your pot is not merely a container, but a canvas of possibilities as well, harmonizing with the proportion and form of your tree. The art of pruning is a delicate dance that shapes and refines your tree while allowing it to flourish and thrive simultaneously. Then, we delved into the world of wiring, spiraling elegant sweeps and graceful curves into your tree. Last but not least, we took a look at new beginnings and dipped our toes into propagation from seeds, cuttings, and nursery stock.

All of these aspects play a pivotal role in the transformation of ordinary plants into extraordinary miniature worlds. Each step is a testament to your patience and skills. Embrace the rhythm of the seasons and grasp the fundamentals to witness the enduring beauty of nature unfold before your eyes.

For now, let's forge ahead into the realm of maintenance.

5
Maintenance

It has been rather evident thus far that when it comes to the art of bonsai, it's not just about chucking a plant in some great soil and hoping for the best. This art form needs not only time but dedication.

This is where regular maintenance and care come into play. It's just as important to maintain your tree's vitality throughout as it is to prep and prime its environment. The art of bonsai is a continual journey, a magical wonder that continuously flows and changes with the seasons. Yes, this all sounds beautiful, but there is a flip side to this story. Things can go wrong, and your precious tree is susceptible to various pests and diseases. However, maintenance is not all just about keeping pesky pests at bay; it also entails maintaining a proper watering schedule, promptly pruning, as well as timely fertilizing.

5.1 Watering Schedule

What's the cornerstone of any successful plant cultivation? Watering! That's because water is life, and without it, there's no life. Simple, right?

Well, believe it or not, some folks get it all wrong when it comes to this aspect, ending up either drowning their trees or drying them out. Thus, understanding the nuances of watering is a skill of its own. Contrary to what one might think, the small restricted root systems need to be watered more frequently. This is all due to the restricted space the tree is confined to, which limits its ability to self-regulate moisture. One thing that's certain is that there are no hard and fast rules about watering because there are too many variable factors that come into play here. Every species has different watering requirements, seasons come into play, soil, size, and plant health, to name a few.

- **Seasons:** Spring and summer are the thirsty seasons because that's when growth is at its peak. Here, your aim should be to water your tree every day, or at least every other day, to ensure that the soil stays consistently moist. As the seasons roll on and autumn approaches, growth slows down, and watering needs to decrease. Winter is dormancy time, further decreasing your bonsai's watering needs. Generally, factors to consider when it comes to increasing watering are direct sunlight, strong winds, and high temperatures. When you have to decrease your watering intervals, factors such as low temperatures, high humidity, and sunshades come into play. Thus, you need to keep a watchful eye on various aspects when it comes to seasons and watering.

- **Water quality:** Rainwater is the golden standard here, filled with natural minerals and devoid of any harsh chemicals. Alternatively, tap water will do the job, but be mindful of the quality of tap water you have. Some tap water contains high levels of chlorine for instance, which is most certainly detrimental to your bonsai.

- **Quantifying quench:** The aim of the game here is to provide a steady, measured supply. Water until you see it trickling through the drainage holes of the pot, indicative of the root system receiving sufficient water without waterlogging the soil. There is a rule of thumb here, and that's to water your bonsai as soon as you notice that the soil is turning slightly dry. Please note the emphasis lies on the word "slightly." Never ever allow your tree to be bone-dry.

- **Moisture test:** You can simply do the ever-popular finger test to gauge the moisture level of the soil. Pop your finger about an inch deep into the soil. If it feels dry, watering time! If it still feels slightly moist, hold out for a day and test the soil again. Alternatively, you can make use of a moisture meter for more precise readings.

- **Species and growth stage:** Consider the species, deciduous trees require more frequent watering compared to conifers for instance. Young saplings require more moisture than mature bonsais.

- **Size:** In general, larger trees require more water and vice versa. This is because of the size difference in the root systems. The more extensive the root system, you guessed it, the more water is required.

- **State of health:** Keep your eyes peeled for any signs of wilting or yellowing leaves which are indicative of a watering imbalance. It goes without saying that a healthy tree can more effectively retain its water.

- **Soil:** The composition of your soil mixture and your watering schedule requires a delicate balance, as they directly affect water retention capacity. Ensure that your soil allows for proper drainage to prevent waterlogging.

- **Pot:** Your pot size and its drainage capabilities also come into play with regard to watering. The smaller pots tend to dry out quicker. Thus, be sure to regularly do those moisture tests.

- **Adapt:** Your tree is its own little breathing, living entity with its own unique preferences. With so many factors that come into play, you will have to closely observe how your bonsai responds to the watering routine. Remember, always have an open curious mind that is ready to learn and make necessary adjustments.

To properly care for and nurture a thriving tree, you must be attuned not only to your tree but also to your environment. Embrace the rhythms of the seasons, heed the wisdom of the soil, and witness your bonsai flourishing under your devoted touch.

5.2 Pruning Schedule

Now, we've delved into pruning throughout this book, but let me ask this: How exactly do trees grow? This question holds significance because comprehending the growth patterns of trees equips you with valuable insights for more effective bonsai pruning.

Let's introduce a new term: 'apical dominance.' This concept signifies that the central stem of a tree holds a dominant role in its growth, overshadowing the development of other branches. This natural mechanism ensures that trees grow taller to avoid being overshadowed by competing counterparts. While it's a survival strategy, it leads to the eventual decline of lower and inner branches, with the top branches taking precedence. This isn't in alignment with the aesthetic goals of bonsai, which is why pruning becomes crucial to counteract the effects of apical dominance.

In essence, it's prudent to focus on more thorough pruning of the top and outer sections of your tree. This strategic approach redirects growth towards the lower and inner areas, achieving the desired bonsai form and balance.

5.2.1 Why Prune?

Why exactly do we prune? Let's recap.

- **Size and proportions:** The art of bonsai is all about creating the illusion of a large, mature tree in miniature form. Thus, managing the size and proportions is key in this journey because it allows you to control the height and width of your bonsai. With a regular bonsai "haircut" you can maintain this harmonious aesthetic.

- **Unwanted growth:** Now, your idea and nature's idea about where branches should grow differ vastly when it comes to your bonsai. Nature often delivers unwanted shoots and twigs. As mentioned, pruning allows you to remove these little "surprises," redirecting energy toward the areas you want to focus on.

- **Branch structure:** Are there branches growing too close together? Perhaps you see that some shoots are stronger than others? Take a step back and observe your bonsai to selectively prune and pinch accordingly. This allows you to guide the growth, ensuring your bonsai develops an elegant and balanced branch structure.

- **Back-budding:** Back-budding is the process of counteracting apical dominance, stimulating new growth closer to the trunk. This allows you to encourage the development of new shoots, which contribute to fuller, more compact foliage.

5.2.2 Timing

You've guessed it! It's all about the seasons again. Generally, the best time to prune outdoor bonsais will be during the growth season which is from early spring right through to late fall. Indoor bonsai trees can be clipped and snipped year-round.

Let's touch base and revise.

- **Spring:** This is the new growth period and pruning during this time is perfect for redirecting energy for stronger, healthier buds.

- **Summer:** Go a bit lighter on the pruning and focus on light maintenance and light pinching new shoots instead.

- **Autumn:** During this time, growth starts slowing down. Thus, prune and refine your tree's shape to prepare it for the winter dormancy period.

- **Winter:** Pruning should be absolutely minimal during the dormancy period. Only cut away dead branches and leaves to keep your tree well-maintained.

5.2.3 Consideration Summary

We have taken a dive into how you go about pruning your tree with prior reading. Let's pull together a quick summary of some key considerations you should take to heart before picking up those shears and snipping away.

- **Species**
- **Growth stage**

- **Size**
- **Health state**
- **Soil quality**
- **Pot size and drainage**
- **Wind, humidity, and temperature**

It's not just about timing when it comes to pruning, you need to give it some careful consideration as well in order to sculpt your tree into the masterpiece you envision. And remember, it should always reflect the harmony of nature, just in miniature form.

5.3 Fertilization

This is the secret sauce in the realm of bonsai: fertilizer! This is your little tree's own energy boost. So, let's recap the nitty-gritty of fertilizing.

- **When:** Spring and summer are feeding time! Generally, every two to four weeks depending on species is a good gauge.

- **How often:** With fertilizer, sometimes less is more. Over-fertilizing can bring forth unhealthy growth spurts, and you don't want that. It's all about balance. Thus stick to regular intervals applicable to the seasons.

- **How much:** Don't be too heavy on the hand with fertilizer, your tree is living in a confined space, making it more sensitive to nutrient levels. Read those instructions, and when in doubt, play it safe and opt for a slightly diluted dosage instead.

- **The best:** The spice of life is variety and fertilizer fits well into this statement. Look for one that has a relatively balanced N-P-K ratio (that's Nitrogen, Phosphorus, and Potassium). These are just the primary nutrients your bonsai needs, not a chemistry class.

- **Application:** Always follow the instructions, and make sure the soil is moist before adding fertilizer to allow even distribution of nutrients.

- **Winter:** This is dormancy time and you should most certainly ease off on the fertilizer. Remember, your tree is in a rest period, thus it doesn't require as much fuel compared to other seasons. You may fertilize once every six to eight weeks.

- **Considerations:** Different trees have different needs, and you have to understand your species' appetite. Deciduous trees have different needs compared to conifers, and tropical varieties also have their own appetites.

- **Patience:** After fertilizing, you need to give your tree some time to digest the secret sauce, allowing it to work its magic. Avoid temptation and steer clear from over-fertilizing. In this case, less is truly more.

Once you get the hang of it, you'll be fertilizing and nurturing your tree like it's second nature.

5.4 Diseases and Pests

Giving your bonsai the greatest care possible means not only giving the optimum soil composition, assuring proper watering, adequate fertilization, and adequate light but also keeping diseases and pests at bay. Oh yes, a healthy tree is a happy tree.

Nevertheless, infestations and diseases aren't exclusive to unhealthy trees, although they do make them more susceptible. Even healthy trees can succumb to these issues. Let's delve into what you might encounter and the measures you can adopt to protect your bonsai from diseases and pests.

5.4.1 Fungal Infections

The unfortunate truth is that fungi are a rather regular occurrence, thus it's important to understand some of the most common types and their signs and symptoms, as well as treatment. Let's dive right in.

- **Anthracnose/Various fungal species**

    o Symptoms: Dark, sunken lesions on the leaves.

    o Causes: The fungus infiltrates leaf tissue and wet conditions such as rain or overhead watering may even further spread these fungal spores, promoting infection.

    o Treatment: Proper sanitation practices, such as removing infected leaves, as well as fungicidal sprays with active ingredients like copper or neem oil can help ward off anthracnose.

- **Brown Rot/Various Monilinia species**

    o Symptoms: Water-soaked and soft infected tissues with brown, decaying spots on flowers or fruits, generally accompanied by a foul smell.

    o Causes: Warm humid conditions come into play again.

    o Treatment: Fungicidal treatments may be necessary during fruiting seasons in general. Prompt removal and disposal of contaminated fruit, as well as sanitary procedures, are other strategies that help in the control of brown rot.

- **Canker Diseases/Various fungal genera**

    - Symptoms: Discolored, sunken lesions on trunks or branches which are generally accompanied by dieback of affected areas.

    - Causes: Canker fungi generally infect trees by entering damaged tissues such as wounds or natural openings in the bark.

    - Treatment: Removing infected parts by pruning affected branches back to healthy tissue in conjunction with applying fungicidal treatments can help manage canker diseases. Prevention is better than cure, thus, proper wound care after pruning is always necessary.

- **Damping Off/Especially species such as Pythium and Rhizoctonia**

    - Symptoms: Sudden death, collapsing, and wilting of seedlings or young plants.

    - Causes: Damping off fungi thrive in overly wet soil conditions.

    - Treatment: Providing proper aerated, well-draining soil can help prevent damping off. In severe cases, fungicidal drenches should be used.

- **Leaf Spot/Various fungal species**

    - Symptoms: Dark, circular spots on the leaves of the tree.

    - Causes: Yet again, a leading cause is humidity which creates the perfect environment for fungal growth within leaf tissues.

    - Treatment: Fungicides with appropriate active ingredients, such as chlorothalonil, can be used to manage leaf spot, along with regularly removing and disposing of infected leaves.

- **Leaf Yellowing/Various fungal species**

    - Symptoms: Generalized yellowing of leaves.

    - Causes: The disturbance of nutrition uptake induced by fungal infections affecting roots causes leaf yellowing.

    - Treatment: Correcting nutrient imbalances and improving soil health can help alleviate leaf yellowing. Fungicidal treatments may be necessary to address underlying fungal infections.

- **Needle Cast/Various fungal species**
    - Symptoms: Browning and premature shedding of needles.
    - Causes: Needle-cast fungi prefer moist conditions, thus, releasing spores during wet conditions, spreading infection.
    - Treatment: Proper and timely pruning and disposal of infected branches can help manage needle cast in conjunction with fungicidal sprays that contain active ingredients like chlorothalonil or copper-based compounds.

- **Powdery Mildew/Erysiphe species**
    - Symptoms: Leaves and stems have a white powdery substance.
    - Causes: High humidity and moderate temperatures are the leading causes. This fungus does not require water on the leaf surface to germinate, making plants in indoor environments or areas with high humidity a lot more susceptible.
    - Treatment: Fungicides containing active ingredients like sulfur, neem oil, or potassium bicarbonate. Proper ventilation and a reduction in humidity levels are also pivotal.

- **Root Rot/Armillaria and Phytophthora species**
    - Symptoms: An unpleasant odor that is generally accompanied by wilting, yellowing, and stunted growth.
    - Causes: Waterlogged soil with poor drainage, all thanks to the fungal pathogens causing root decay.
    - Treatment: Address your watering schedule and be sure that your soil allows for proper drainage. Systemic fungicides that target root pathogens, such as Fludioxonil, Thiophanate-Methyl, and Propamocarb, can also be applied.

- **Rust/Various fungal species**
    - Symptoms: The presence of rusty pustules and sores on the stems and leaves of the tree.
    - Causes: Overly damp environments are the general cause as this is conducive to his type of fungus.
    - Treatment: Removing infected plant material and practicing good sanitation along with fungicides containing active ingredients like sulfur or copper can help control rust.

- **Slime Flux/Various bacterial and fungal species**

    o Symptoms: Oozing, foul-smelling liquid with a slimy appearance from wounds or openings in the trunk.

    o Causes: It often occurs in weakened or stressed trees with wounds and may be caused by a variety of different fungi and bacteria.

    o Treatment: Cleaning and sealing wounds, which are part of basic wound care, are preventative strategies for slime flux. These bacterial infections may also be treated with systemic antibiotics.

- **Sooty Mold/Various fungi, especially Ascomycetes**

    o Symptoms: Black, powdery substance on leaves and stems, generally with a sticky honeydew secretion. A lot of the time sooty mold develops in conjunction with pests like aphids.

    o Causes: The excretions of sap-feeding insects, like aphids, scale insects, and mealybugs, create an ideal environment for sooty mold fungi to thrive in.

    o Treatment: Insecticidal soap or neem oil to control the pest and insect environment may contribute to the prevention of sooty mold. Pruning and disposing of heavily infested branches should immediately be conducted.

5.4.2 Pests

Oh those pesky pests, however, dealing with them is just another part of the game. After all, what are you going to do? Banish all the critters from the great outdoors to safeguard your precious tree. Impossible I say! However, focus on what you can do. Stay vigilant and know your enemies. Learn more about them, and put preventive measures in place.

- **Ants**

    o Detection: Presence of ant trails around the base or on the tree.

    o Causes: Ants farm aphids and scale insects for their honeydew, which leads to secondary pest issues.

    o Treatment: Remove any ant colonies near the bonsai, and apply ant barriers such as ant bait stations.

- **Aphids**

    o Detection: Presence of small, soft-bodied insects on stems and leaves.

- Causes: Deformities and weakening of the tree, such as curly leaves and distorted growth, are caused by the aphids feeding off the plant saps.
- Treatment: Insecticidal soap and neem oil are helpful options. Alternatively introducing natural predators like ladybugs, is another consideration.

- **Borers**
    - Detection: Sawdust-like frass around entry points caused by boring small tunnels or holes in the branches and trunk.
    - Causes: Borers are beetle larvae that tunnel into the wood and cause structural damage to the trunk and branches of the tree.
    - Treatment: Remove affected branches, apply insecticidal soap or neem oil, and destroy any infected wood.

- **Caterpillars**
    - Detection: Presence of caterpillars on the tree.
    - Causes: Caterpillars feed voraciously on foliage, potentially defoliating the tree.
    - Treatment: Use insecticidal soap or neem oil and handpick caterpillars from the tree.

- **Fungus Gnats**
    - Detection: Larvae found in the soil and adult gnats flying around the tree.
    - Causes: Fungus gnat larvae feed on plant roots, causing severe root damage.
    - Treatment: Allow the soil surface to dry between waterings and make use of yellow sticky traps to catch adult gnats.

- **Japanese Beetles**
    - Detection: Visible metallic green beetles.
    - Causes: Adult beetles feed on foliage causing severe damage, and leaving leaves skeletonized with only veins remaining.
    - Treatment: Apply insecticidal soap or neem oil and handpick beetles from the tree.

- **Leaf Miners**
    - Detection: Presence of small, fly-like insects around the tree.
    - Causes: Leaf miner larvae tunnel through leaves creating distinctive patterns, leaving blotches and serpentine tunnels on the leaves.
    - Treatment: Apply insecticidal soap or neem oil and remove and destroy the affected leaves.

- **Mealybugs**
    - Detection: Cottony, white masses on leaves and stems.
    - Causes: Mealybugs feed on plant sap weakening the tree, stunting growth, and causing yellowing of leaves.
    - Treatment: Remove visible insects with a cotton swab soaked in alcohol, then apply insecticidal soap or neem oil.

- **Scale Insects**
    - Detection: Tiny, immobile bumps or scales on leaves and stems.
    - Causes: Scales attach themselves to the plant and feed on sap, causing yellowing and stunted growth.
    - Treatment: To get rid of scale insects, promptly prune heavily infested areas and apply insecticidal soap or neem oil.

- **Snails and Slugs**
    - Detection: Presence of slimy trails.
    - Causes: Snails and slugs feed on leaves, causing cosmetic damage such as holes in leaves.
    - Treatment: Apply diatomaceous earth or use slug pellets and handpick snails and slugs from the tree.

- **Spider Mites**
    - Detection: Yellowing, a stippled appearance, and fine webbing on leaves.
    - Causes: These pests feed on sap by piercing plant cells which in turn causes damage to the tree.

- o Treatment: Dislodge the mites with a strong jet of water and use neem oil or insecticidal soap.

- **Thrips**
    - o Detection: Visible small, slender insects.
    - o Causes: Thrips feed on plant tissue, causing scarring, stippling, and distorted growth.
    - o Treatment: Apply insecticidal soap or neem oil. Alternatively, introduce natural predators like ladybugs.

- **Vine Weevils**
    - o Detection: Presence of C-shaped grubs in the soil and notched edges on leaves.
    - o Causes: Vine weevil grubs feed on the roots, causing significant damage such as wilting and stunted growth.
    - o Treatment: Use insecticidal soil drenches for adult weevils and apply nematodes to the soil.

- **Whiteflies**
    - o Detection: Small white insects in flight.
    - o Causes: Whiteflies feed on plant sap and can cause yellowing leaves, leaf drop, sticky honeydew, and stunted growth.
    - o Treatment: Use insecticidal soap or neem oil and introduce natural predators like ladybugs.

5.4.3 Viruses and Bacteria

In the miniature world of bonsais, where every little leaf and twig holds significance, viruses, and bacteria pose a silent threat. Viewed as microscopic invaders, they remain unseen to the naked eye, yet the disruption they can cause should not be overlooked.

Contrary to bacteria, viruses are not considered living organisms. Comprising a protein coat housing genetic material, viruses rely on a host cell to replicate. These viral infections in bonsais manifest in various ways—mottled or distorted leaves, stunted growth, and abnormal growth patterns are all indicators. These symptoms make it a rather tricky endeavor to identify a viral presence, as it mimics the same symptoms of various other stressors. At the end of the day, it's all about keeping the basics in check, such as using clean tools, providing proper nutrition, and maintaining a healthy environment.

Then we have the single-celled critters: bacteria. Some are beneficial, while others, well, not recommended at all. Harmful bacteria bring a laundry list of problems such as foliar diseases, root rot, or cankers. To steer as clear as possible from any bacterial infections, ensure proper watering practices, disinfection of tools, regular inspections, and employ organic mulches that are great deterrents when it comes to the proliferation of harmful bacteria. You can even introduce more beneficial microorganisms such as mycorrhizal fungi to fortify your tree's defense.

Bonsai care undoubtedly requires a hands-on approach and precision. Every gesture shapes its unique form from watering, strategic pruning, fertilizing, and guarding against pesky pests and diseases. So be sure to be diligent and keep your eyes peeled for any unwanted guests, growth, or stress to your tree.

5.5 Revitalizing Tips

So, your bonsai is busy wilting and dying? Well, the cold hard reality is that something is wrong, aside from pests and disease, it could all also boil down to human error. Now that you have a fundamental understanding of the basics of bonsai care and cultivation, saving and reviving your tree is merely an action plan that contains all of this knowledge condensed together in chronological order. All you can do is follow these steps, keep a close eye, and hope for the best in all honesty. Let's take a look.

Assessment

- **Visual inspection:** Thoroughly examine your tree for any signs of distress, such as wilting leaves, discoloration, spots, fungal growth, or pests. This includes inspecting the soil.

- **Soil inspection:** Assess the moisture level of the soil, making sure it's not waterlogged or too dry.

- **Root inspection:** To thoroughly investigate the roots, you will need to gently remove the tree from the pot. Diseased roots exhibit symptoms such as being brown in color, mushy, or having a foul odor.

- **Environmental inspection:** Look at the light exposure, humidity levels, and temperature and be sure that they all align with the tree's specific requirements.

- **Water inspection:** Assess your watering practices by evaluating your watering methods and schedule. Both over and under-watering lead to stress and root rot.

After conducting this thorough assessment, it would be best to start fresh and repot from the beginning. Completely remove your tree from its current environment to ensure that it is free of any factors that have or might still leave it vulnerable, enabling it to have a proper fresh start.

Repotting Procedure

- **Potting:** Start with the general potting preparations as per some prior reading

- **Remove old soil and roots:** Working through the roots with your root rake or comb, remove any diseased or dead roots and any excess soil from the roots.

- **Trim leaves and branches:** Cut away any dead or diseased branches and leaves with sterilized pruning shears.

- **Position your tree:** Place your tree at the same depth as before in the new pot, and then add your soil as usual, ensuring all air pockets are eliminated.

After Repotting

- **Watering:** Water thoughtfully to be sure that all the soil settles properly and all the excess water is drained out.

- **Environment:** Place your bonsai back into a suitable environment with the appropriate temperature, light, and humidity levels.

- **Monitor:** Regularly check in with your tree to monitor the progress and see if there are any further adjustments required.

- **Care:** Provide consistent care and patience for reviving a bonsai tree is a timely process.

These are all steps that you're familiar with, however, adhering to them will give your tree the best chance at recovery and survival. Should you need it, some expert advice and a guiding hand will most certainly also be worth the time and effort.

6
Unlocking the Extraordinary: Elevate Your Bonsai Skills With Advanced Techniques—Your Exclusive Gift Inside!

Ever heard of Jin and Shari? No, these are not any personal friends of mine, however, they hold something truly extraordinary. These techniques have the power to manipulate the very look of a tree. Mastering these advanced techniques, such as working with deadwood, for instance, demands skill and finesse. And this is merely the tip of the iceberg!

Are you ready to try your hand at these truly fascinating advanced techniques? Well, you're in for a treat, because I've got an incredible surprise just for you! Consider this your golden key to unlock a world of wonder!

7
A Wish From the Author

Here you have it, beloved fellow bonsai enthusiast, a whole story filled with invaluable insights and techniques to kickstart your adventure in cultivating your magical miniature world! It's not just a tree, it's a living piece of art, a testament to your time and devotion. But, it doesn't just end there!

The profound connection it fosters with nature, discovered through nurturing and tending, mirrors the depths of our own existence. You are weaving a tale, a legacy that has the ability to live on longer than the hands that cultivate it. Isn't that something rather awe-inspiring?

Yes, sure, the art of bonsai requires knowledge, however, the most profound lessons are taught by the tree itself.

The time, care, patience, and nurturing that you put into it establishes a deep harmony within you, imparting wisdom within you. This tree is not just an ornament, you'll find that it's also one of the best teachers you'll ever encounter.

Thus, truly lean into it and hone your craft, dedicate yourself. You have the ability now, and you undoubtedly deserve to be part of something truly magical: witnessing life unfold right before your very eyes!

I would be honored if you would share your honest feedback in support of the effort and passion poured into this book. Your ideas, insights, and reflections might even inspire the growth of another bonsai-inspired creation from my side!

Book 3.

Classy Bonsai Display | From Home Elegance to Eternal Fame

Showcase Indoor and Outdoor Your Bonsai as Modern Art and Master the Criteria for Competition Excellence

Kazuo Hanabusa

1
Introduction

Allow me to let you in on a little secret: bonsais are meant to be seen and admired. Yes, you have to display and showcase their beauty and your craftsmanship. Cultivating and caring for your bonsai is only one half of the story, formally displaying is the other part that allows your tree to be fully appreciated. Never for a moment believe it's just about placing them on a pretty pedestal. No, it completely transcends that. You are crafting an ambiance with your display that should communicate through each and every object present in the display, right down to the minutest details. And when it comes down to showcasing your bonsai, it's truly all about the details.

Thus when it comes to choosing items for your display, it really requires some good consideration and planning to ensure that everything merges together in one harmonious arrangement.

Now, to truly excel in the art of bonsai display you will have to possess a firm grasp on all the elements involved including display stands, tables, accent plants, rocks, poles, companion objects, and environments. And let's not underestimate the importance of carefully selecting the ideal shape, size, and symmetry of all these elements to further enhance the cohesion of the display. Here's another little secret I can tell you: It's not a secret that the sense of pride that comes with displaying your "grand finale" masterpiece for others to admire is absolutely undeniable!

Irrespective of whether you're a seasoned pro who exhibits collections at conventions or in shops, or a passionate hobbyist who prefers displaying in a more intimate, personal setting, having the perfect backdrop and cohesion is pivotal.

Let's take a closer look at some of these aspects.

2
The Importance of a Good Bonsai Display

Now we have briefly touched on some of the important aspects of display, but I would prefer if we could hone in on each separately to get those creative gears turning. Another reason for getting those creative gears turning is that when it comes to displaying your bonsai, every placement should be intentional; nothing should be left as an afterthought. It's a miniature world reflecting your patience, dedication, and creativity, not a salad side order.

- **Setting the stage:** Displaying your bonsai isn't just about finding an empty corner that needs to be filled. Rather it resembles a multi-faceted choreographed dance composed of various elements. Each of these elements has a distinct characteristic that contributes to the overall symphony of your display. There is more to it than meets the eye and every detail contributes its own significance.

- **The elements:** The performers in your display generally consist of display stands that set the stage. Then there are the accents, poles, and rocks akin to supporting acts, adding dimension and depth to your story. Your companion objects harmonize the elements, adding that final finishing touch to bring your picture to completion.

- **Shape, size, and symmetry secrets:** This is precisely where the magic resides, in the details. Every element - the shape of your stand, the symmetry of your accents, and the size of your table - all have a hand to play when it comes to creating that perfect spot where form meets function and beauty harmoniously meets practicality.

- **Pride and joy:** It's not solely about having absolutely every single element present in your display, it's about orchestrating them into perfect harmony. Each piece should elevate each other, collectively elevating your miniature tree into a living work of art. Right here is where the sheer joy and satisfaction lie.

2.1 Styles

Style is another crucial consideration. This aspect serves as the foundation for your entire creative sphere. And, with such a broad choice of styles at your disposal, there's bound to be one that perfectly matches your own taste and preferences while also complementing your environment. So what exactly are your options?

- **Formal exhibition display:** This is akin to a red carpet event in the world of bonsais where highlighting the individual beauty of each tree is the aim of the game. This entails well-lit spaces with bonsais all meticulously placed and displayed on striking stands.

- **Informal home display:** Say hello to free reign when it comes to creativity with these kinds of displays. It's all about you and finding spaces around your home to showcase your bonsai. Whether it's a windowsill, a corner table, or even a specially designed bonsai shelf. It's all about seamlessly integrating your bonsai into your living space.

- **Landscape display:** With these displays, you are mimicking nature by arranging multiple bonsai, rocks, and other elements. Ultimately you are creating a little world in tiny trays like a miniature mountainscape or a fantasy forest.

- **Outdoor garden display:** This style is all about the great outdoors. creating a natural setting in your garden or yard. It generally involves placing your bonsai among rocks, other plants, or even alongside a small water feature to create a natural backdrop for your bonsai in your garden.

- **Seasonal themes:** Some folks like to keep things fresh and interesting by switching their displays up according to the seasons. Why not? You could have a spring display with blossoming trees for instance, or even a winter display with evergreens and some seasonal accents.

- **Tokonoma display/traditional formal display:** The tokonoma, a traditional Japanese alcove, is where a thoughtfully chosen bonsai is displayed alongside other complimentary elements such as scrolls or pottery, harmoniously blending nature and art.

- **Workshop displays:** As the name states, these displays showcase your work in progress. When you're part of a bonsai club or workshop, you display your tree along with others to get feedback and learn new techniques.

Here are all the important basics! That's most certainly more than enough to get excited about what's to come, right? Let's not stop raising our levels of excitement now; let's hone in on the foundations and factors of bonsai display.

2.2 Foundations of Bonsai Display

What does your bonsai deserve? A setting that's as magnificent as its form! So what are you going to do?

The choices you make in displaying a bonsai are rooted in a variety of factors. Some of these factors are deeply intertwined with scientific principles. Let's work through some of these influences, and look at some aspects to take into consideration.

- **Bonsai Type:** Know your species, it's the first rule of bonsai, applicable to pretty much anything - cultivation, maintenance, and display alike. Your tree's genetic makeup guides its display, Coniferous trees, for instance, prefer cooler environments, which make them more preferable for outdoor displays. Tropical species, on the other hand, are more susceptible to cold temperatures, making indoor options for displays.

- **Environment:** The environment dictates the conditions for your tree's growth, and it's no different when it comes to displaying your bonsai. As you are aware by now indoor settings offer more control over conditions where you can regulate temperature and light. This significantly reduces external stressors due to fluctuations compared to outdoor environments. However, the plus side of outdoor displays is the fact that they harness the dynamic energy of nature. This setting aligns with the tree's evolutionary disposition, enabling your tree to undergo more natural seasonal changes crucial for its long-term vitality.

- **Seasonal Showcase:** Understanding your seasons and how they affect your tree with regard to growth surges and dormancy is yet another aspect that comes into play.

Adapting your display to mirror these seasonal shifts honors both your tree and nature's inherent rhythm, adding depth to the overall aesthetic. Remember, nothing on display is an afterthought, it's all meticulously planned.

- **Harmony in Diversity:** It's more than just aesthetic appeal when it comes to accents and companion plants. These elements contribute to a harmonious microenvironment through allelopathy. Allelopathy is a magical, natural phenomenon where plants release chemicals that influence the growth of any neighboring plant. This is a beautiful interaction that contributes to a balanced ecosystem within your miniature world.

- **The Art of Patience:** What happens every time you prune your tree? You trigger hormonal responses within your tree which increases the auxin concentration. This is a plant hormone that is responsible for apical dominance that shapes the tree's growth pattern. Therefore, it's important to consider pruning in relation to apical dominance when planning your display.

- **The passage of time:** Age is beautifully etched in a bonsai's growth rings, each ring representing a year of the tree's life. This is known as a dendrochronological record, which provides you with a glimpse into the tree's history. By considering the age of the bonsai, one can tailor the display to honor its unique journey.

- **Cultural influence:** In Japanese bonsai traditions the naturalistic integration of the tree with its environment is oftentimes emphasized. This reflects a reverence for nature deeply rooted in Shinto beliefs. As you can notice with this example, the cultural backdrop against which a bonsai is displayed will significantly impact your chosen style.

- **Personal connection:** If you display a bonsai in a manner that not only reflects but also resonates with your personal style, it will foster a sense of connection. And it's not a secret that interactions with nature have a significant positive effect when it comes to the reduction of stress. Thus keep in mind that your display should instill a sense of peace and calm within you, otherwise you might as well just put up a Christmas tree instead.

- **Trial and error:** The art of bonsai encourages you to experiment and adapt. Every adjustment leads to a deeper understanding of the intricate interplay between your tree, your care, and the environment. It's a fascinating endeavor that merges together artistry, horticultural expertise, and scientific understanding. Through amalgamating these factors, you craft a display that you are not just showcasing your patience and dedication, honoring your tree's intrinsic beauty, but you are also paying homage to the natural world from which it draws its essence.

- **Display Tables:** This is your crafting foundation, and they come in all different shapes and sizes. You can opt for natural stone slabs or for a more elegant touch, wooden stands will do the trick. Your choice will most certainly impact your display aesthetic. On the other hand, the table dimensions and material composition also influence moisture and temperature levels, which directly impact your bonsai. Don't let that fact slip your mind.

- **Display Stands:** This element is responsible for elevating your beautiful presentation, serving both functional and aesthetic purposes. But it's not just about the height and design that you should be concerned about here, remember your stand height also impacts the airflow around your tree.

- **Accents:** This is how you add to your bonsai's story: accents. These are generally things such as rocks, stones, or miniature figurines that are all carefully selected and placed within your display. If you want depth, texture, and context, accents would be the way to go, guiding the viewer's gaze and creating a harmonious visual experience.

- **Companion elements:** Companion elements are usually things such as plants, mosses, or small bodies of water that contribute to creating a micro-ecosystem within your display. This is an ecological approach that beautifully captures the intricate relationships found in nature. These tiny elements all contribute to various aspects such as nutrient cycling and humidity levels, each in their own special little way.

- **Scrolls and backgrounds:** Scrolls and backgrounds offer a visual narrative that provides depth and context to the display, which strongly influences the viewer's perception of your tree's proportions, aesthetic, and form.

- **Lighting:** As you know, light influences photosynthesis and growth of any living plant, including your bonsai. Whether it be natural or artificial light, your display should be illuminated to showcase its full splendor while still receiving an adequate amount of light at the same time.

- **Containers and Pots:** I most certainly do not have to delve into the importance of choosing the perfect pot again. You are already fully aware that your choice of pot should harmonize with your tree and complement your overall display.

- **Personal Style:** A very important aspect of your display is that it should also reflect your own individuality. At the end of the day, it is an expression of your own personal taste. Are you eclectic, minimalistic, or more of an innovator? Lean into your style and embrace the stage of your miniature world.

- **Understanding perspective:** I saved this idea for last for a reason: we will most surely be expanding on it. What's your tree's phototropic response, or its tendency to grow toward the light? You need to position your tree in a way that maximizes light exposure in your display, ensuring balanced growth and making it more visually appealing. Then there's apical dominance which also plays an important role. The apical bud, the uppermost bud of a bonsai, is the boss when it comes to exerting hormonal control over lateral branches, inhibiting their growth. You need to maintain this natural growth hierarchy by displaying the best side of your tree.

Your selection, consideration, and arrangement of all these elements is a pure art form in itself. Through delicately balancing aesthetics, functionality, and horticulture your awe-inspiring display is accentuating the inherent beauty of your tree and creating and emphasizing the wonders of our natural world.

2.3 Understanding Perspective: A Viewer's Angle

Don't make your tree look like a bonsai, make your bonsai look like a tree. – John Naka

They say that beauty is in the eye of the beholder, and that is most certainly true. It's all about perspective, my fellow enthusiast because perspective is the gateway to art's true essence.

Our eyes are the lenses we see through, unlocking subtle nuances and hidden dimensions through our perspectives. This makes it important to understand and choose your angles well when it comes to your display. You need to play your best angle to showcase your intention, craft your narrative, as well as invite and direct gazes to focal points. It's not about simply creating a visual, it's about creating an experience that will transform an observer into a participant through delivering an enriched encounter.

Here's a couple of questions for you to consider.

- **Viewing angle:** What is your primary viewing angle going to be? This is the angle that should display your tree's best features.

- **Natural vs. designed perspective:** Do you want a natural perspective that mimics how a tree will be seen in nature, or would you prefer a designed perspective where you specifically highlight certain features?

- **Eye-level vs. above-level:** How will your bonsai be viewed, from eye level or above eye level? Eye-level displays tend to be more intimate compared to the broader view of above-eye-level displays.

- **Focal points:** What are the most striking features of your miniature marvel? Perhaps it's the trunk curves or unique branch formations. You need to identify these features and make sure that they're prominently visible because they are the different focal points of your tree.

- **Balance and composition:** Does your display fit harmoniously? Assess the overall balance and composition from the chosen perspective and make adjustments where you feel the visual flow is interrupted.

- **Background and surroundings:** Is there anything in the environment that could distract from your bonsai's features? Assess the background and surroundings of the display and adjust as needed.

- **Negative space:** Does the negative space around your tree enhance or overwhelm your display? Negative space is essential, but it should not be the focal point, thus make adjustments to bring forth the desired balance to your display.

- **Consider the viewer:** Put yourself in the shoes of your audience. What will the first impression be? How will the perspective change as you move around the tree? Question yourself about all these little nuances.

- **Trial and error:** What's your most engaging viewpoint? Do you need to change things? What can be improved? What can you learn? Trial and error, that's how we all learn. Be patient with yourself and enjoy the journey.

- **Highlighting front, back, and side perspectives:** Do you know the graceful front of your tree? The intriguing back? The captivating side views? Paying attention to the details of every angle is necessary to create a complete visual experience.

- **Ensuring accessibility:** Is your bonsai easily visible? Make sure your tree is easily accessible and at a comfortable viewing height for a personalized experience where it can be appreciated up close.

2.4 Companion and Accent Plants

Companion planting and accent plants work wonders when it comes to stepping up the aesthetic game of your display. Each plant should complement and enhance the beauty and charm of your miniature world. Let's take a look at some pointers.

- **Create a sense of scale and depth:** Accent plants are like your supporting act in the show, enhancing the narrative, and adding depth to the overall display. Remember, they always have to complement your tree's style and size. They have to harmonize with your bonsai's aesthetic. This will require you to consider factors such as leaf color, shape, and growth pattern.

- **Contrasting foliage or flower colors:** If you want a dynamic, vibrant display you need some visual contrast. Opt for accent plants with foliage or flower colors that stand out against the bonsai.

- **Cultural requirements and growth habits of companion plants:** For harmony to prevail, compatibility is essential. Thus, your companion plants should share the same environmental needs as your tree. This ensures they can happily flourish together without any visual or growth-related concerns.

- **Micro-ecosystems:** Companion plants can transform your display into a thriving community! Regulating humidity levels, improving nutrient cycling, and even sheltering some beneficial insects. Everything you need to have your own mini-ecosystem!

- **The art of Ikebana:** Ikebana, the art of Japanese flower arrangement, is a tremendous source of inspiration since it emphasizes mindful selection. This means that each and every plant contributes and serves a purpose.

- **Different textures and forms:** Variety is the spice of life! Make use of the different textures and forms of accent plants. This makes for a far richer sensory experience.

- **Growth rates:** Be sure that you understand the growth rates of your accent plants, it should always be compatible to maintain the desired balance of your display.

- **Seasons:** Keep the seasons in mind. Well, we always have to keep the seasons in mind when it comes to bonsais. Choose companion plants that harmonize with the changing textures and colors of your tree. This will make for a seamless, ever-evolving display.

2.5 Suiseki/Viewing Stones

Suiseki, a traditional Japanese art form, involves appreciating naturally formed stones that have been weathered into all sorts of beautiful shapes, resembling landscapes, rivers, animals, mountains, or other objects in nature. This practice is very closely related to the art of bonsai, as they both have a common goal: aiming to capture the essence of nature in a miniature form.

Let's take a look at how you can use the Suiseki when it comes to incorporating stones and other elements into your display.

- **Selecting Suiseki:** When it comes to stones for your display, look for nature's little sculptures that embody the essence of a miniature landscape. This includes looking at aspects that have fascinating shapes, colors, and textures.

- **Positioning in relation to your tree:** Consider the size and shape in relation to your tree, they should enhance and not overpower your tree or, your overall display.

- **Scale and proportion:** Suiseki should always be in proportion to your tree. Smaller stones are preferable for more petite trees and larger ones for bigger trees. It's all about finding that perfect balance and harmony.

- **Reflecting natural landscapes:** Choose stones that reflect the environment you want to portray. Smooth stones may present a tranquil lake, and jagged stones may present rugged mountains for instance.

- **Texture and surface:** Focus on the texture and surface and how that interacts with the senses. How does the surface of the stone interact with light? And what kind of sensory dimension would the texture evoke?

- **Visual flow:** Suiseki should guide the gaze, from your tree to the stone and back to your tree again. It's like a visual dance, a melody to follow with the eyes.

- **Contrast and complement:** The color of the stones also plays a significant role. Smooth pale, smooth stones could mirror your bonsai's graceful lines, and dark, rugged stones may beautifully juxtapose a delicate bonsai in bloom.

These are just some basics to get you started. However, creativity, in itself, knows no bounds. Creating your display, although there's a lot to consider and much to learn, is a very personalized process. It has to be, in order to create a unique masterpiece that's a reflection of your inner world.

Another important aspect that you should never forget is to always find enjoyment in it. After all, that's why you embarked on this journey in the first place.

3
Display Ideas for Your Bonsai

Now that you understand the significance of presentation in the art of bonsai, let's dive in and look at where and how you can display your bonsai. There will undoubtedly be a suitable location for your miniature world, whether indoors or outdoors.

3.1 Indoors

Where can you put your bonsai indoors? Well, pretty much anywhere, as long as it ticks all your bonsai's requirement boxes keeping your tree happy and healthy.

Let's do a brief rundown.

- **Living room:** Placing your bonsai in the living room allows for easy viewing, a great conversation starter, and a vocal point for the decor. A special piece of nature right in the heart of the home.

    - Positioning: A good spot for placement would be on any prominent surface such as a dedicated display stand or your coffee table, as long as it's easily visible.

- **Dining Room:** A perfectly placed bonsai can add elegance and a serene atmosphere for meals in your dining area.

    - Positioning: The center of the dining table is the obvious go-to, but don't overlook that buffet either.

- **Home Office:** Placing a bonsai in your office is perfect for reducing stress and enhancing focus, providing you with a more tranquil work environment. We all can do with a touch of nature amid our deadlines and work responsibilities.

    - Positioning: Your desk is the answer here, as long as it doesn't obstruct your work area. However, depending on your office furniture, you can place it anywhere, as long as it's in your line of sight to catch a calming glimpse whenever needed.

- **Bedroom:** The perfect piece of peace for your bedroom. Your bonsai can create a serene atmosphere in your ultimate sanctuary, promoting tranquility and relaxation.

    - Positioning: As with every space in the house, as long as it's within line of sight and doesn't obstruct any movement. You can opt for the dresser, place it on a bedside table, or even a dedicated display stand.

- **Kitchen:** Perfect for form meeting function! Placing your bonsai in the kitchen will bring a sense of freshness into the space.

    - Positioning: You can opt for your kitchen countertops or shelves.

- **Bathroom:** Here you need to choose carefully because your tree should be able to thrive in humid conditions to transform your bathroom into a relaxing oasis.

    - Positioning: As long as your tree is placed in an area with indirect light, such as a windowsill or a small dresser.

- **Entryway/hallway:** What a warm, mesmerizing welcome when placed in the entryway! This is a great placement to set a positive tone for a warm atmosphere.

    - Positioning: You can place it on your console table or an eye-catching stand. Be very mindful of the traffic here though.

- **Staircase Landings:** Perfect for a focal point on those landings where we're always unsure of what to do.

    o   Positioning: A sturdy stand or display table will do the job.

- **Sunroom/conservatory:** With ample sunlight and controlled humidity, this might just be one the best spots for your bonsai.

    o   Positioning: A table or any other sturdy surface will suffice, as long as it receives indirect light, especially during the hottest times of the day.

3.1.1 Special Spots

Remember, the spot you choose in any room indoors serves as a backdrop for your display. Thus proceed with caution. You wouldn't want to miss the whole aim of the game here, which is to create a harmonious visual. You certainly wouldn't want it to resemble a local fairground.

- **Window sills/bay windows:** Window sills and bay windows are perfect spots with the flood of natural light they provide.

    o   Positioning: The window sill is the obvious go-to, however, a stand, or a console is placed in front of the window. Whichever you choose, be sure that your tree doesn't obstruct access to the window or your view. Placement and positioning of your tree in any spot should always be practical and functional.

- **Floating Shelves:** This is a very magical, modern, and minimalist option to display your tree. It's particularly well-suited for compact living spaces, allowing you to conserve floor space, as opposed to using a stand or console, for example.

    o Positioning: Your bonsai should always be easily viewed. Thus, your floating shelves should be at eye level or slightly above. When installing them, keep in mind the weight of your bonsai to ensure your floating shelves are securely fastened.

- **Wall-mounted nooks:** Wall nooks are typically designed to transform empty wall spaces and awkward nooks into more functional areas. Incorporating a bonsai into a wall-mounted nook creates a captivating, natural focal point that enhances both the functionality and visual appeal of the space.

    o Positioning: As long as the spot has sufficient light, whether it be natural or artificial. Height, as with the floating shelves, is a factor here. Be sure your bonsai is placed at a visually comfortable height.

- **Kitchen Countertops:** What better to add to your culinary display than a piece of greenery? Placing your bonsai on your kitchen countertop is a perfect example of how you can blend natural elements with functional aspects.

  o Positioning: Avoid direct exposure to heat or steam, and ensure your bonsai doesn't interfere with meal prep to prevent any unwanted accidents.

- **Mantelpieces:** Always an elegant centerpiece on a mantelpiece, drawing attention to the focal point of the room.

  o Positioning: You can place it anywhere that's aesthetically pleasing on the mantelpiece, as long as it's stable and won't be accidentally knocked over.

- **Bookshelves:** Positioning your bonsai among books and other decorative elements provides a fresh perspective, transforming it into dynamic displays that demand attention and invite exploration.

  o Positioning: Eye level is the answer and also be sure not to crowd your tree with other objects.

- **Coffee tables/side tables:** Conversation starter smack-bang in the middle of social interactions. A bonsai on a coffee table undoubtedly always makes for a magical focal point.

    o Positioning: The center of the table provides the ideal spot, offering a complete 360-degree view, provided it doesn't hinder the functionality of the table.

3.1.2 Decoration Tips

Shelves/Elevated Spaces

Once your bonsai is placed on those shelves, they're not just mere storage units anymore, they are transformed into a canvas of your display. They hold a pivotal role in achieving the sought-after harmony. Thus, I deem it more than fitting to delve into some essential tips covering additional shelf decor.

Materials and Aesthetics

All chosen elements should harmonize with your interior. Factors like color, texture, and style should all be given thought to create a harmonious, cohesive look

- **Wood:** Go no further if you're looking for something that would harmonize with the organic essence of your miniature tree and exude a timeless appeal. Wooden shelves such as cedar, oak, or walnut are your go-to. And, for a rustic touch, live-edge wooden shelves will be perfect with its irregular edges and one-of-a-kind quality.

- **Glass:** For smaller, more compact spaces, glass shelves are the top choice due to their transparent quality, drawing focus directly to the tree.

- **Metal:** If you're leaning more toward the modern, contemporary side of life, metal shelves offer a minimalist feel. This sleek option will provide a magnificent contrast to the organic nature of your tree.

- **Customized shelving:** Nothing wrong with stepping things up a notch and customizing your shelving to perfectly accommodate your miniature marvel, ensuring more seamless integration.

- **Hidden lighting:** For some added ambiance, install LED strip lighting underneath your shelves. This creates a beautiful, subtle glow along the lines, highlighting your tree's features like its contours and foliage.

Light and Positioning

A word of caution when it comes to light, steer clear from extremes! This means that any harsh direct sun and harsh artificial light should be side-stepped to avoid any unnecessary damage or stress to your bonsai. Remember, everything in the world of bonsai is about finding that perfect balance.

- **Artificial light:** Not enough natural light? No problem, you can employ LED lights to mimic that natural glow.

- **Natural light:** Bathe your bonsai in natural light by positioning your shelves close to windows, skylights, or sliding doors.

- **Lighting fixtures:** For a gentle downward glow illuminating your bonsai with warm, inviting tones, consider adjustable spotlights or pendant lights above shelves.

- **Light filters:** To filter out harsh, direct sunlight, use blinds or sheer curtains. This will diffuse the intensity of sunlight and protect your tree from any excessive, damaging light exposure.

- **Adjustable shelving brackets:** Another great hint is to adjust shelving brackets that can be adjusted in height. This enables you to raise or lower shelves as you please to achieve the perfect lighting conditions for each bonsai as required.

- **Revolving shelving units:** Rotating shelves is yet another clever consideration that will enable you to twist and turn your tree's position for optimal lighting.

- **Shelving arrangement:** Arrange your shelves diagonally or in a zigzag pattern to add a touch of visual interest. This is also a clever way to ensure that your miniature marvel receives the optimal amount of light.

- **Mindful Positioning:** I have said it, and I will say it again, eye level is the way to go because it creates a more intimate experience when it comes to viewing your bonsai.

However, this is just a general rule of thumb. Positioning is all dependent on each individual's taste, vision, and environment.

Seasonal Variations

Roll with the seasons and rotate your displays to showcase the ever-evolving beauty of your tree. And here are some insights on how you can go about successfully doing so.

- **Winter:** Accents that are minimalist and display icy tones will provide an elegant, crisp look to carry through the winter theme.

- **Spring:** As spring fills the air with its fresh, vibrant blossoms, incorporating lighter, livelier accents will align perfectly with the cheerful ambiance of the season.

- **Summer:** Here you want robust and lush, accentuated with tiny props that reflect the summer sun like miniature garden furniture for instance.

- **Autumn:** A display of hued leaves, complements autumn with earthy-toned elements for an inviting, warm atmosphere.

- **Multi-tiered displays:** Displaying more than one bonsai? Make use of tiering when you create distinct levels for different seasonal bonsais for some added depth and dimension.

- **Seasonal backdrops:** You can make use of backdrop elements such as wallpapers of fabrics behind your display shelves that you can easily swap out to complement the changing seasons.

Props and Other Elements

Each display is a creative opportunity for you to freely express yourself through creating a multi-dimensional visual experience. Thus, experiment with various different arrangements and combinations of accents and props around your tree to find that sweet spot that resonates with your personal style, vision, and sense of harmony.

- **Books:** You can never go wrong with books in life. And, what better to use than books to tell a story in your display? Choose books with exquisite covers and complementary hues, or books about poetry, bonsai, or Japanese culture, for example.

- **Candles:** Candles are ideal for creating a captivating atmosphere. You have a wide range to choose from—scented or unscented, and an array of colors that can enhance your display. Just be mindful and always safely position your candles, or better, use flameless LED candles.

- **Bamboo Accents:** Another way to embrace Japanese aesthetics is through the integration of bamboo elements. Bamboo mats, vases, or screens will all complement a serene minimalist nature.

- **Scrolls:** Embrace tradition by hanging scrolls that feature nature-inspired motifs, beautiful landscapes, or ancient Japanese calligraphy.

- **Prints and posters:** Bring in some artistic depth to enhance your display's visual narrative by incorporating prints with depictions of nature.

- **Stones:** We've already delved into the significance of stones for that grounding touch in your display. Arrange them around the base or create an intriguing collection around your bonsai to replicate a natural landscape.

- **Crystals and gemstones:** Pull some energy into your display by making use of crystals and gemstones. You have amethyst, rose quartz, and turquoise to name a few. The options here are truly endless.

- **Trays and plates:** Frame your scene with decorative trays or plates with interesting designs to complement your overall aesthetic.

- **Figurines:** Little figurines such as small animals or symbolic statues to evoke some sentiment are yet another great way to contribute to your narrative. Be thoughtful and strategic with your placement to evoke a sense of movement and liveliness.

- **Miniature furniture:** This is an excellent way to add a touch of miniature surrealism: incorporate tiny benches, bridges, or pagodas. Just ensure that the scale of your miniature furniture aligns with the rest of your display to pull through that magical, whimsical atmosphere.

- **Seasonal ornaments:** Celebrate with the seasons by adding seasonal ornaments to reflect each season. Items like pine cones, seashells, and acorns are a great start.

- **Infusing Fragrance:** Embrace the sense of smell by adding an elegant incense burner or fragrance diffuser for an added delicate, aromatic layer to your display. This should of course be something subtle in smell such as cedarwood or lavender for instance.

Bases and Platforms

Ah, the bonsai stage—bases and platforms. It's somewhat similar to attending a concert, isn't it? The ones with a touch of creative finesse tend to be much more captivating and visually engaging than the standard kind. It's no different when it comes to your bonsai. So, let's explore some creative tips to elevate your bonsai's stage.

- **Materials and aesthetics:** Nothing we have overlooked thus far when it comes to materials, but let's have a quick recap specifically regarding the stage.

- **Wooden:** Wood is always your go-to for that natural, rustic, organic feel. Look at different textures and grain patterns for a customized feel.

- **Metal:** Industrial, modern, and contemporary, this element is perfect for a striking contrast with the organic nature of your bonsai.

- **Stone:** To align with the ethos of bonsai, stones give that sense of added groundedness and stability. Shaped river stones, slate, or granite are all examples that will provide a sturdy, compelling foundation.

- **Ceramic:** Glazed or unglazed, it's all up to you. Ceramic options are versatile in colors, surfaces, and pattern designs. You can opt for something that will contrast or match your tree's aesthetics.

- **Bases and platforms:** When it comes to these aspects, you have to think about shape, height, and overall design.

- **Flat bases:** For added stability and simplicity, flat bases ensure your bonsai is the star attraction. They always work well with pretty much any style or shape of the tree.

- **Slab bases**: Whether it's a stone slab or a carved wooden slab, they can be custom-fitted to the contours of your bonsai for a seamless integration and a grounding, rustic aesthetic.

- **Multi-level platforms:** Tiers and stepped platforms add multiple dynamic dimensions and depth. This is a great option if you are using multiple bonsais in your display or for accent elements.

- **Trays or saucers:** Yes, their primary function is to catch water. However, trays and saucers also contribute to the overall aesthetics of the display. Enhance them with gravel or sand as a clever way to infuse a Zen garden ambiance.

- **Creating a mini Zen garden:** If you hear Zen garden, you immediately think of balance and tranquility. And you're right! Incorporating raked sand and meticulously placing stones into your display brings with it a contemplative charm. And here's how to do it:

    - *Choose a suitable tray:* Shallow rectangular trays are a great option in general for this aesthetic. But you are free to choose any shape or size that best suits your vision.

    - *Fill:* Fill your tray with a layer of fine sand or gravel, spreading it evenly across the tray, laying the foundation of your Zen garden.

- *Position stones:* Simply position your stones strategically into the sand. Be mindful though and consider the balance and visual flow when you create your clusters of interest or sanded patterns.

- *Rake the sand:* To rake the sand you can use a small rake, even a toothpick will do the trick. Create ripples or any other natural pattern.

- **Complementary plants and decorations:** Your display does most certainly not need to be confined to your tree alone. You can enhance your visual impact and expand your story by adding complementary elements.

- **Moss:** For a lush, forest floor vibe moss is your answer. This beautiful green carpet-like feature brings such a beautiful ambiance to any display.

- **Accent plants:** Expand on your miniature garden with accent plants such as ferns or succulents. As long as they are compatible with your display and have similar requirements as your bonsai.

- **Miniature figurines:** As mentioned, including miniature furniture, these elements add that magical touch of whimsy to a display. .

- **Lanterns and ornaments:** Lanterns and other ornaments can be brought in to enhance a specific cultural aesthetic.

3.2 Tokonoma

What's Tokonoma displays? Curious, aren't you? Well, curiosity never truly killed any cat, allow me to share.

Tokonoma displays are a quintessential element of Japanese aesthetics. They are alcoves, typically found in Japanese-style reception rooms, dedicated to showcasing cherished items, often featuring a central bonsai. These spaces are meticulously curated, seamlessly integrating elements of nature, craftsmanship, and artistry. Just like any bonsai display, the bonsai is positioned alongside complementary elements, such as scrolls or pottery, creating a harmonious environment. It's a breathtaking arrangement characterized by simplicity, capturing serenity, and balance, and evoking contemplation and appreciation.

3.2.1 Bonsai Tokonoma Styles

A corner of sheer elegance and artistry, in the heart of a Japanese home, where simplicity beautifully merges with sophistication. Let's briefly dip our toes into the world of Tokonoma displays. However, proceed with caution because you will undoubtedly allocate a room in your house to this endeavor!

- **Zen Tokonoma:** Let's kick off with the familiar! Devoid of any unnecessary adornments to instill a deep sense of contemplation, the Zen Tokonoma allows the mind to breathe. The ever-present bonsai, perhaps a scroll, or a stone or two, you are submerged in reflection and introspection upon entering this space.

- **Shoin style Tokonoma:** A case of less is more, the Shoin style stands as a magnificent embodiment of Japanese architectural principles. It is a true masterpiece of precision. Every single element is thoughtfully and meticulously positioned to craft a visual symphony that celebrates the art of minimalism. Here, harmony and balance merge to create a space that breathes life into the essence of Japanese design.

- **Tea Ceremony style Tokonoma:** Steeped in a world of tea traditions, here simplicity, yet again, reigns supreme. The showstoppers generally include a flower arrangement, a scroll, and a bonsai to create an atmosphere of peace and tranquility, setting the stage for a sense of appreciation.

- **Suiseki Tokonoma**: You are well-familiar with Suiseki by now. Thus as the name states the Suiseki Tokonoma is a stage for viewing the awe-capturing beauty of naturally formed stones. These stones, sculpted by nature's hands of time, are generally placed alongside a bonsai, creating a poetic amalgamation of human craftsmanship and nature's timeless artistry.

- **Seasonal Tokonoma:** Seasons are evidently a big feature in the world of bonsais, and when it comes to Tokonoma decor this is a significant factor when it comes to the transformation of decor. During autumn you may step into more earthy tones compared to the vibrant hues of a spring setting. This not only pays homage to nature's ever-evolving tapestry but also imparts a sense of continuity to the home.

- **Modern Tokonoma:** Tradition meets evolution in this instance where the classic concept takes a modern twist. Infused with contemporary flair, the use of unconventional materials and abstract art serve as examples that attest to our ever-changing world.

- **Nijo Tokonoma:** Embodying the more refined taste of the upper-echelon samurai class, the Nijo-style Tokonoma exudes a sense of noble sophistication. With a display of ornate ceramics, intricately woven tapestries, and, of course, a bonsai, you step into a world of timeless grace and aristocratic elegance.

- **Niju Tokonoma:** Why settle for less in life if you can have the best of both worlds? Also referred to as the double Tokonoma, it features two alcoves, each with its own theme. Generally, these two separate themes complement each other, allowing for more creative expression and creating a symphony of artistry.

- **Nara Tokonoma:** Paying homage to Japan's ancient capital, Nara during the Nara period, from 710 until 794 AD, it features elements that evoke the spirit of a bygone era.

Elements such as ancient ceramics, antique scrolls, and bonsais honor the rich cultural Japanese heritage that still continues to inspire to this day.

It's rather evident that when it comes to cultivating and displaying your bonsai indoors, it's more than just merely placing it in a pretty corner. No, my fellow enthusiast, there is some serious thought required here for you to create that ultimate balance and achieve the perfect harmony. However, with these insights, you will be well on your way to "nesting" the perfect spot for your miniature marvel. Hey, perhaps you might even end up with a little renovation project to introduce a Tokonoma-style nook in your space. Who knows?

3.3 Outdoors

Oh the great outdoors! And what better way to enhance it than with a spectacular bonsai display?

The style of display outdoors is just as important as its indoor counterpart. From meticulously curated gardens to untamed gardens that mimic untouched nature, the possibilities at your disposal are yet again truly endless. May I say though, with outdoor displays your options of elements are a lot more diverse compared to indoor displays. This is great news because a broader array of options allows for a more expansive and engaging story to be displayed.

3.3.1 Display Spaces

Before we delve in and look at some great tips and ideas for your outdoor bonsai display, let's just tie down a few fundamentals. If you want your outdoor bonsai display to be long-lasting, you will have to take a couple of factors into consideration first. This will include compatibility with neighboring plants, understanding the space, and taking aspects such as navigation into account. Additionally, it's important to check off the usual suspects such as enough light, temperature, seasonal changes, and humidity.

- **Water-side:** One of nature's most powerful elements, water, yet it exudes tranquility in its presence at the same time. For many, it's the perfect spot for contemplation and, ironically, reflection. Having your bonsai near water, such as a koi pond for instance, not only beautifully merges the elements of earth and water, but also amplifies the tranquility of both your tree and the water element.

    o Positioning: One big factor when positioning your bonsai near water is to be sure that no roots would incur any water damage. A great way to overcome this minor obstacle is to elevate it by placing your tree on top of a stable, water-resistant pedestal.

- **Rock garden:** As water compliments the tranquility of your tree, natural rock elements complement the resilience of your tree. Generally, rock gardens are rugged in nature which makes for an interesting dynamic contrast between the organic nature of your bonsai and the solidity of the textured stone.

- - Positioning: Your tree should most certainly blend with the rocky environment, and to further urge this cause you can arrange additional rocks to mimic natural stone or rock formations. Additionally, you may add some moss as a final touch to soften the starkness.

- **Garden alcoves:** Alcoves, those special little nooks in an environment, with their sense of enclosure create an intimate feel that strongly emphasizes the miniature world of your bonsai. Aside from this, they also provide protection from harsh elements, making them more than ideal for an outdoor display.

  - Positioning: Keep the proportions of the space and the size of your tree in mind. You would not want the space to swallow your tree or vice versa. And the rest is history as they say, as the general environmental factors should evidently be taken into consideration, not only here, but with every chosen spot.

- **Garden borders:** Garden borders form beautiful frames for outdoor living spaces, offering structure and a more organized display of the environment. Placing your bonsai, or bonsais to create an entire bonsai border, will make for a beautiful, natural flowing transition between neighboring flora.

  - Positioning: Achieving a harmonious balance between spacing and foliage is crucial in this context. It's important to avoid overcrowding the layout, allowing for generous pathways and access for close-up viewing.

- **Pergolas:** As with alcoves, pergolas offer great protection from the elements for your bonsai. The vertical display of pergolas adds an extra dimension to perspective, creating a more layered and visually appealing display.

  - Positioning: First thing first, you don't want to place your bonsai within a wobbly pergola, risking your miniature world to come crashing down. Thus, make sure it's a sturdy structure. You can even incorporate hanging plants to further emphasize the vertical dimensions.

3.3.2 *Display Designs*

Great! You have found a spot! But how shall you display it? On the ground, a table, perhaps a chair? Oh no, that will most certainly not suffice, it's a display after all.

At the same time, you don't have to shoot the lights out and construct an entire empire for your tree.

Let's take a look at a few simple solutions to make your trees stand out in the great outdoors.

- **Benches and tables:** As with plinths and vertical poles, benches and tables are utilized to elevate your bonsai to offer a structured, dynamic visual.

  o Positioning: Scale is a factor with benches and tables outdoors as much as it is indoors. Keep it in relation to the surrounding elements for a harmonious aesthetic.

  o Materials: Wood, stone, concrete, and metal.

- **Vertical poles and plinths:** Going up? Vertical elements draw the eye upward, this is great for adding dimension and height to any display. Poles and plinths at eye level isolate the object, making it a focal point.

    o   Positioning: You will need a strategic hand and eye when it comes to placing these aspects in your garden, ensuring you maintain that perfect balance while still sparking visual interest. Always be sure that your plinths and poles are securely anchored and stable.

    o   Materials: Wood, stone, and metal.

- **Vertical wall displays:** This is most certainly a personal favorite! Perfect for maximizing space in compact gardens, vertical wall displays offer a magnificent, unique backdrop for your bonsai.

  - Positioning: Best to be sure that the wall is sturdy enough to carry the weight of your installation, especially if it includes multiple bonsais or other potted plants. Pick a wall that is easily visible, turning it into a focal point with your vertical wall display.

  - Materials: Wood, stone, metal.

- **Terracing:** Through terracing you create visually pleasing layers, creating a beautiful interplay with dimension and depth by showcasing your bonsai/s or other plants at different heights.

    o   Positioning: Good drainage and effective sunlight is key here. You don't want plants overgrowing each other and negatively impacting the overall health of your bonsai.

    o   Materials: Stone, wood, and concrete.

- **Natural features:** Using what you have, such as boulders or rocks, gives that extra touch of originality, allowing for a more natural flow of your landscape.

    o   Positioning: Whatever object you choose, be sure that it complements your display, not overwhelm it.

    o   Materials: Rocks, logs, and boulders.

4
Feng Shui and Bonsai

The art of Feng Shui and the art of Bonsai, what a power couple! But why are these two art forms rather deeply intertwined and often practiced together? Well, my fellow enthusiast, as sure as the sun rises and falls every day and the moon as well, it's all about balance and tranquility. Yes, it's all about finding that harmony and inner peace.

Feng Shui is rooted in ancient Chinese philosophy and it's all about harmonizing the flow of energy in a space to promote holistic well-being and instill a perfect sense of harmony. And as you are aware, bonsai, derived from Chinese Penjing, shares this profound connection between our human environment and nature. Think of them as cousins born from the same principle.

Place your bonsai strategically, which is what is always required in the art of bonsai, and you are embodying the very essence of Feng Shui! Let's say, for instance, you opted to place your bonsai in the east of your house, you have represented family and health according to the principles of Feng Shui. Rather magnificent isn't it? It's like getting two for the price of one!

This interplay is further stretched into the interpretation of your bonsai's shape. A bonsai that is upright in nature emanates powerful, vibrant energy. A cascading style bonsai, on the other hand, will channel a more calming energy for instance. Both these art forms have another commonality—placing emphasis on harmony and balance. When you prune your bonsai to create a perfect well-proportioned tree that seamlessly merges with its environment, you are essentially echoing the intention behind feng shui—creating a space of harmony and balance.

This is a purely symbiotic relationship and a true dynamic partnership, where both equally enhance each other's purpose.

You are becoming a seasoned bonsai enthusiast now, my fellow enthusiast, with the wealth of knowledge you have accumulated thus far throughout our journey. And what an enriching beautiful journey it is! Now that you have a solid overview of the principles of display, indoors and outdoors, let's move on and dive into the world of competition. After all, a little competitiveness never harmed anyone.

5
Online and Offline Bonsai Competitions

There's been a big surge in the popularity of bonsai competitions in recent years, captivating enthusiasts from all corners of the globe and all walks of life alike. Don't think for one moment you will be walking into an event that is akin to walking into a normal nursery filled with mere greenery. No. These gatherings are extravaganzas. Grand showcases of sheer mastery where you can witness the finest artistry, skill, and creativity. But, what exactly is adding fuel to this competitive bonsai fire? Different strokes for different folks as they say. For some it's an opportunity to showcase their artistic flair, others simply want to push their own mastery boundaries, and then there's the folks that simply want to dip their toes into the waters of their own horticultural prowess.

Irrespective of the reason, online and offline bonsai competitions are an opportunity for everyone. You can gain feedback, expert advice, knowledge, accolades, recognition, and a wider audience with your mindfully crafted and meticulously nurtured creations. Above all, it offers a chance to connect with like-minded people and build a camaraderie that flourishes, fostering a sense of community and belonging.

These events inspire you to refine your skills and techniques, experiment, explore, and innovate. It's not just about your bonsai, my fellow enthusiast, it reaches far beyond that. It forms a part of self-improvement and personal development as well.

In this chapter, we are going to nose-dive right into the fascinating world of bonsai competitions. We'll be touching on various aspects such as what judges look for, presentation, transport, and etiquette, as well as how to find and engage in Bonsai competitions.

5.1 Judges

Nobody likes to be judged, but in any competitive environment, you have to keep your head and heart open and take it as constructive criticism. Having said that, what exactly do judges look for in bonsai competitions?

For starters, judges, in general, are seasoned professionals who are on the lookout for various aspects, such as craftsmanship and artistry seamlessly merging together, as part of their evaluation. They have a wealth of experience and a discerning eye to match, making sure only the best rise to the top. Let's step into their world with a little checklist to prepare you for what's to come.

- **Overall design and composition:** It's all about checking the harmony box. Judges look for a harmonious balance between all elements within a display. This includes a tree, container, and any other added extras. The key here is to evoke a sense of balance and natural beauty.

- **Health and vigor:** Unhealthy, wilting plants are strictly prohibited. They want to see a testament to your skill reflected in the vitality of your bonsai. It has to flourish, be well-maintained, not a pest in sight, and boast a wealth of healthy foliage.

- **Nebari/surface roots:** Oh, the nebari, a bonsai gem! Not only does your nebari have to be functional and lend appropriate support, but it also has to be sure as fire has an aesthetic appeal to it in the world of bonsai competition. It's all about spread and radial symmetry for the judges.

- **Ramification and foliage pads:** Ramification is all about the carefully controlled growth of foliage along branches. Foliage pads are all about the massing of leaves on a branch. Good ramification is defined by fine branching, and adequate foliage pads should be well-defined and dense, all appropriately scaled to your tree.

- **Trunk:** Your backbone, the trunk, is going to get a close examination from the judges. Its taper, movement, and surface texture should all exhibit a gradual decrease in diameter as it ascends.

- **Branch structure:** Your branch structure should be well-distributed. No bare spots and no overcrowding, they should radiate from the trunk in a balanced fashion.

- **Container selection:** Containers will always be a factor in the art of bonsai, competition or not.

- **Horticultural aspects:** Even what can't be seen by the naked eye gets judged! Your soil composition, watering regimen, and seasonal care will be evaluated because they all directly reflect the vitality of your tree.

- **Artistic expression and innovation:** This is where it gets personal because it's all about your unique style and creativity. Judges appreciate innovative approaches, so best you push those creative boundaries.

- **Attention to detail:** From wire placement to surface refinement, judges scrutinize every fine detail. Nothing is left unchecked. However, keep in mind that it's these fine details that elevate a bonsai from good to exceptional.

5.2 Presentation

The presentation of your bonsai is a direct reflection of you! That's the cold, hard truth. Entering the competitive arena when it comes to bonsai, a meticulously prepared presentation makes all the difference, showcasing not only the aesthetics of your tree but also your attention to detail and commitment to the art form.

Here's a lovely little checklist for you to get started.

- **Cleanliness and grooming:** Your bonsai has to be spotless. Free from any dust and debris. Be sure to trim, refine, and clean up every nook and corner of your tree and display.

- **Container aesthetics:** Yup, the container issue again, you know the song. It should enhance the overall aesthetic, not overshadow it. It's not a container competition.

- **Nebari display:** Showcase at an angle that allows for ease of visibility. Nebari should always radiate from the base of the trunk, indicating stability and vitality.

- **Soil surface and top dressing:** To even out and neaten your soil surface, consider using dressings such as moss or gravel to kick up the visual appeal with a notch or two.

- **Accent plant or companion:** The same principles apply here as with pots: it should complement, not overpower the overall composition.

- **Scroll or display stand:** The key in competition - complement, not overpower. Choose carefully when it comes to these added extras, they should add depth and remain within the context of your presentation.

- **Backdrop and setting:** A clean uncluttered backdrop is the safest bet to ensure your tree remains the focal point of your display.

- **Lighting considerations:** For judges to see and appreciate every feature, make sure your tree is well-lit. If needed make use of artificial lighting that's strategically placed.

- **Info and labeling:** Be concise and accurate about your bonsai's information. This includes aspects such as species, age, and special cultivation techniques.

- **Safety and stability:** Ensure that the bonsai is securely positioned, well-balanced, and stable, to prevent any accidents during the display.

- **Seasonal considerations:** Always keep the seasonal context of the competition in mind to highlight the bonsai's features in relation to the time of year.

5.3 Competition Etiquette

Competition is a powerful driving force that can bring out extraordinary results. – Unknown

Manners do make the man or the woman. Always be sure to read and understand the competition's rules and guidelines beforehand. This will contribute not only to a more positive experience but atmosphere as well. Here are some fundamentals, but please take note that they may differ from competition to competition.

- **Register in advance:** A stitch in time saves nine. It's always better to register and complete all necessary paperwork and payments before the event. This will allow you to focus on more important aspects such as refining your display.

- **Arrive early:** Be punctual. Arrive earlier, this not only shows respect but will give you an opportunity to settle in and calm those nerves.

- **Respect the rules:** Know and understand the rules of each competition you enter. On top of all, follow them. These rules include aspects such as tree size, presentation requirements, and style to name a few.

- **Be mindful of space:** Respect the space of others. Be wary that you are not blocking displays, and avoid overcrowding of family and friends. There needs to be consideration and flow, not just for your creation to be seen and admired, but those of others as well.

- **Tidy area:** Always be sure that your display area is spotless. Remember, everything gets scrutinized and judged.

- **Respectful discussion:** Always avoid any form of negativity, even if at times, it means you have to grin and bear it. Every engagement should be respectful, even complaints.

- **Permission for photos:** Always ask for permission before taking photos of someone else's work. Some artists might find it offensive, thus, be mindful before you start snapping away.

- **Practice patience:** Always be patient with the entire process, whether it's waiting to be judged, results, or taking pictures. This will save you a whole lot of unnecessary frustration.

- **Respect the judges' decisions:** Accept the judges' decisions, whether you win or not, it is what it is. Rather learn from the experience instead of showing dissatisfaction.

- **Participate in award ceremonies:** Show your appreciation by participating in award ceremonies and celebrating with others.

- **Clean up after yourself:** Ensure that your area is clean and tidy before leaving. Dispose of any trash or unwanted materials responsibly.

5.4 Transportation

You can't just pop your tree in a sturdy box on the backseat, strap it in, and hope for the best. You need to be sure that it will arrive in the same pristine condition as when it left your care.

Here's your guide!

- **Plan the route:** Planning the route ahead of time will help ensure you are able to travel along the roads with the least resistance. Avoid sudden stops and rough terrain as much as possible.

- **Appropriate container:** Be sure that your container houses your bonsai safely and is fitted with a non-slip material. The container itself should be sturdy and well-fitted, irrespective of which material you opt for.

- **Pot padding:** To prevent movement or damage, wrap your pot in a protective cover such as bubble wrap or foam.

- **Secure your bonsai:** Soft ties or raffia will do the trick to gently secure the branches of your bonsai, ensuring they won't sway or break during the journey. Additionally, be sure to cushion any delicate foliage.

- **Nebari and root check:** Ensure that the surface roots are also protected and secure. If necessary, add some extra soil to the pot to provide additional stability. You can always brush it off afterward when you do your fine tweaking.

- **Ventilation and protection:** Be sure that your bonsai has adequate ventilation and protection from extreme cold or wind during long journeys. Breathable covers such as cheesecloth or mesh will do the trick.

- **Labeling and information:** Attach a label with your contact information and any specific care instructions for the bonsai if you are making use of a special courier.

- **Secure the container:** Double-check that containers are all closed properly.

- **Transit stops:** Make pit stops to periodically check on the bonsai during transit to ensure everything is still secure and in good condition.

5.5 How to Compete

Exciting times are on the horizon when competing in bonsai competitions. There's so much to gain.

But where do you find and join these extravaganzas? Let's look at some reliable methods for you to hunt down these resources.

- **Bonsai club websites:** Hunt down some reputable bonsai club websites in your local area. You'll undoubtedly stumble across a competition or two there in their listings.

- **Online forums and communities:** The wonders of our modern world, bringing bonsai enthusiasts together, thank our lucky stars! Delve in and engage with like-minded people on forums and social media to get the low-down on what's happening with regard to upcoming events and competitions.

- **Social media platforms:** Follow prominent bonsai artists, clubs, platforms, and organizations for regular updates on any upcoming events. There's Twitter, Facebook, Instagram, and TikTok, it's truly endless and you have it all at your fingertips.

- **Bonsai publications:** These magazines regularly feature advertisements and articles about upcoming competitions. You don't even need to purchase a magazine, most of their websites also provide valuable information in this regard.

- **National and international bonsai organizations:** Organizations like the American Bonsai Society (ABS) or the European Bonsai Association (EBA) maintain event calendars on their websites, listing competitions and exhibitions around the world. Google is your friend!

- **Botanical gardens and arboretums:** These institutions often host bonsai exhibitions and competitions as part of their horticultural events, contact them directly for event schedules, or do regular check-ins on their websites.

- **Local nurseries and bonsai suppliers:** Do you want regional info about anything green? These are probably some of your best bets when it comes to bonsai competitions in your region. They often have information about regional competitions and may even sponsor or participate in these events. Best you make friends with a couple of managers.

At the end of the day, news spreads like wildfire, you just have to follow the smoke to find the flame, and in our modern-day society, it truly isn't rocket science.

Here you have it, my fellow enthusiast. Nothing can stop you now. The thought of entering the competitive arena might seem overwhelming at first, however, you have more to gain than what you have to lose in reality.

When you're ready, I would most certainly encourage you to embark on at least one of these adventures.

6
A Gift to You: What Do You Want to Know?

What great timing! Your special surprise has just arrived! Just like I promised, and, of course, in line with all the incredible knowledge you've gained so far, here's a little slice of magic just for you! Why? Well, firstly because you earned it and you deserve it! And secondly, with all that wisdom you've gained, I am sure you have a lot of questions swirling around in your head. Thus, I jumped ahead in time and compiled a list of FAQs, specially crafted to expand on your expertise!

Simply download the QR code provided and you're ready to go! You will broaden your horizons and delve into a world of knowledge that's both everyday and unusual, but most certainly bound to leave you inspired.

7
Conclusion

There are only two ways to live your life. One is as though nothing is a miracle. The other is as though everything is a miracle. – Albert Einstein

Let's commend ourselves for successfully completing another leg of this spectacular journey! Of course! Navigating through all those technical aspects, you've probably noticed that our journey has become increasingly conversational.

My fellow bonsai enthusiast, it was indeed imperative that we establish the grit, rules, and principles of this art, presenting them in a clear and straightforward fashion to provide you with a fundamental understanding without any blurred lines.

Afterward, my friend, we can sit back and enjoy the growth. And this is the time! I would like to emphasize that if, at the beginning, you find yourself feeling flustered and overwhelmed, remember that this book is not a race or a test, it's your guiding companion.

You may revisit any section or chapter as you wish, just like mastering the fundamentals of bonsai, acquiring all this knowledge takes time, patience, and unwavering dedication. What a beautiful combination! No rush here. It's all about you and your own rhythm, just like the seasons.

Please, don't hesitate to share your candid review of the content in this book. All your time, effort, insights, opinions, and reflections are immensely valuable. Even more so, any additional expertise and advice you can offer will be warmly embraced to spread the love of knowledge.

Remember, this is a special journey, you grow with your tree, or trees perhaps! You're an expert, believe in yourself!

Printed in Great Britain
by Amazon